*Finding the Landlord*

ALSO BY KATHRYN LINDSKOOG

*Light in the Shadowlands*
*Fakes, Frauds and Other Malarkey*
*Creative Writing for People Who Can't Not Write*
*The C. S. Lewis Hoax*
*How to Grow a Young Reader*
*Around the Year with C. S. Lewis and His Friends*
*A Child's Garden of Christian Verses*
*The Gift of Dreams*
*Loving Touches*
*Up from Eden*
*C. S. Lewis: Mere Christian*
*The Lion of Judah in Never-Never Land*

# FINDING THE LANDLORD

A Guidebook to C. S. Lewis's
*Pilgrim's Regress*

**KATHRYN
LINDSKOOG**

CORNERSTONE PRESS CHICAGO
CHICAGO, ILLINOIS

© 1995 Kathryn Lindskoog

All rights reserved. No portion of this book may be reproduced without permission in writing from the publisher, except by a reviewer who may quote brief passages in a review.

Published by Cornerstone Press Chicago
939 W. Wilson Ave., Chicago, IL 60640

Printed in the United States of America
98 97 96 95   4 3 2 1

Cover painting by Pauline Baynes, C. S. Lewis's chosen illustrator
Painting used by permission
Cover and book design by Pat Peterson

Library of Congress Cataloging-in-Publication Data

Lindskoog, Kathryn Ann.
    Finding the landlord : a guidebook to C. S. Lewis's Pilgrim's regress / Kathryn Lindskoog ; edited by David Mortimer.
      p.   cm.
    Includes bibliographical references and index.
    ISBN 0-940895-35-8
    1. Lewis, C. S. (Clive Staples), 1898–1963. Pilgrim's regress.
2. Christian fiction, English—History and criticism. 3. Pilgrims and pilgrimages in literature. 4. Mysticism in literature.
5. Allegory.   I. Mortimer, David, 1964–     II. Lewis, C. S. (Clive Staples), 1898–1963. Pilgrim's regress.   III. Title.
PR6023.E926P535  1995
823'.912—dc20                                              95-34102
                                                            CIP

*To John, my fellow pilgrim,
who happened to be born in Fundamentalopolis in
Minnesota exactly twenty days after C. S. Lewis's
John was born in Puritania in 1932.
May their journeys end at
the same crossing.*

I set out to find an Island and I have found a Landlord instead.

—C. S. Lewis

## CONTENTS

Preface   ix
Acknowledgments   xi
Introduction   xiii

book one: The Data   1

book two: Thrill   13

book three: Through Darkest Zeitgeistheim   24

book four: Back to the Road   37

book five: The Grand Canyon   44

book six: Northward along the Canyon   58

book seven: Southward along the Canyon   69

book eight: At Bay   83

book nine: Across the Canyon   92

BOOK TEN: THE REGRESS    100

APPENDIX ONE: THE ESSENCE OF ALLEGORY    115

APPENDIX TWO: REASON AND IMAGINATION:
            TWO HEMISPHERES OF KNOWING    123

APPENDIX THREE: THE YEARS OF THE LIFE OF C. S. LEWIS    131

BIBLIOGRAPHY    135
INDEX    161

# PREFACE

This book is based on lessons given at Saint Andrew's Benedictine Priory, New Orleans Baptist Seminary, New College Berkeley, Fuller Theological Seminary, Chapman University, and Seattle Pacific University. I came to wish that these lessons might take on a more complete and permanent form.

I do not claim that this work contains much which readers could not find out for themselves if, at every allusive or illusive place in *Pilgrim's Regress,* they stopped to do research. I thought the lessons and this book worthwhile because all that individual research seemed to me, as it seems to many others, unsatisfactory. First, readers look for help only when it is obvious that they need help—if then. But there are many aspects of *Pilgrim's Regress* which seem simpler than they are, and readers can benefit from aids they would not have sought. Second, interruptions for research spoil the reading by taking one *out* of *Pilgrim's Regress.* My hope was that an unpretentious little guidebook would lead the reader further into *Pilgrim's Regress* instead. Continually searching through atlases and botanical volumes while surrounded by beautiful

---

This preface is an adaptation of C. S. Lewis's own preface to his book *The Discarded Image: An Introduction to Medieval and Renaissance Literature* (Cambridge: Cambridge University Press, 1964).

scenery spoils your enjoyment of the landscape. But referring to a guidebook along the way doesn't spoil this enjoyment. In fact, it is likely to increase your pleasure by guiding you to features you would have otherwise missed.

There are, of course, readers who prefer to receive from *Pilgrim's Regress* whatever literary experience this book, unaided, may happen to create in an unprepared mind; so there are Americans who mix only with other Americans when they go abroad, who look at other countries as picturesque, and who have no desire to learn what life there is really like for the inhabitants. That is one way of doing it. I have no complaints about people who read *Pilgrim's Regress* in that way; I first read it that way myself forty years ago. But this guide is written for the others.

# ACKNOWLEDGMENTS

Henry Noel, founder of the New York C. S. Lewis Society, did research that has helped those who lack a classical education understand many quotations in *The Pilgrim's Regress*. He made a gift of his work to the public, and I have drawn heavily upon it.

In 1975 Paul Ford, founder of the Southern California C. S. Lewis Society, invited me to lead a one-week workshop for about fifteen people at Saint Andrew's Benedictine Priory, in which we explored *The Pilgrim's Regress* with Henry Noel's notes for reference.

To Henry Noel and Paul Ford I owe the impetus which led to my further learning and teaching and writing about *The Pilgrim's Regress*. Without their influence, I might have missed this prolonged excursion into rare allegorical terrain. Robert L. Hurd, professor of philosophy at Loyola Marymount University in Los Angeles, was a wonderful companion at one point along the way.

To Pauline Baynes, C. S. Lewis's chosen illustrator, I owe great thanks for her encouragement and for her painting on the cover of this guidebook. And to Pat Peterson I owe thanks for his interior illustrations.

Managing editor Jane Hertenstein of Cornerstone Press made this guidebook possible by catching the vision and carrying through. In the end, Jennifer Ingerson and Sally Watkins labored on it as proofreaders, and Tammy Boyd served as researcher and indexer. Best of all, my outstanding editor David Mortimer and his assistant Nanci Mortimer made the polishing a pleasure. Perhaps in fifteen or twenty years Molly Mortimer will take this book down from the shelf and enjoy the fact that her parents started work on it with her in their hearts and finished it with her on their laps.

*On March 31, 1995, I sent Henry Noel a manuscript copy of this acknowledgments section; but the letter was returned because he had moved, and I sought him in vain. In light of his health, there was reason to be alarmed. Henry Noel died on June 14, 1995, without learning of this book and his part in it.*

# INTRODUCTION

## *How John's Journey Came to Be*

When Clive Staples Lewis was two and a half years old, on a vacation at the shore with his mother and brother, he was enthralled by local trains. A highlight of his vacation was visiting the railroad station frequently to see the trains. His mother therefore took him into a shop to buy him a toy train, and the clerk offered to tie a string to it so that he could pull it.

Lewis, a pudgy toddler who then went by the nickname Baby, replied indignantly, "Baby doesn't see any string on the engines what Baby sees in the station."[1]

In a sense, Baby insisted on keeping strings off his engines for the rest of his life. Lewis had an acute desire for reality. *Pilgrim's Regress* is largely the story of his need for authenticity.

Soon an object of greater importance than the toy train came into Lewis's childhood. Lewis tells about it at the begin-

---

1. Flora Lewis to A. J. Lewis, 17 June 1901, Lewis Papers: Memoirs of the Lewis Family 1850–1930, ed. W. H. Lewis, Marion E. Wade Center, Wheaton College, Wheaton, Ill., vol. 11, p. 318.

ning of his spiritual autobiography, *Surprised by Joy*. When Lewis was still very little, his brother Warren once created a toy garden in the lid of a tin cookie box. This toy garden made the child Lewis aware of the beauty of nature for the first time—nature that was "cool, dewy, fresh, exuberant."[2] Because these children lived in Northern Ireland, nature really was cool, dewy, fresh, and exuberant.

The next major incident in Lewis's life turned out to be the key to his life and thus the key to his book *Pilgrim's Regress*. Lewis stood beside a flowering currant bush on a summer day, and suddenly the memory of his brother's toy garden arose as if from centuries ago. The child Lewis was overwhelmed with an enormous bliss beyond description. It was a kind of desire, but before he could know what he desired the sensation was gone. One might think that he desired the beauty of nature or the little garden of long ago, but that was not it. In a sense all his previous short life seemed insignificant after that moment. The currant bush, or what had come through the currant bush, had marked him for life.

A second experience like the first one came to him through the Beatrix Potter book *Squirrel Nutkin*. It shocked and troubled him, not because the naughty squirrel lost his tail to an angry owl, but because it caused him to somehow fall in love with autumn. There was a sense of immeasurable importance about this sensation that came over him. It was different from any other pleasure in life.

The third experience of this emotion for Lewis came from a brief passage of poetry about the Norse god Balder. When Lewis read these few lines of poetry, they created in him a

---

2. C. S. Lewis, *Surprised by Joy: The Shape of My Early Life* (San Diego: Harcourt Brace Jovanovich, Harvest, 1966), chap. 1, p. 7.

desire of almost sickening intensity.

At this point in *Surprised by Joy* Lewis warns anyone who is bored by those three childhood incidents—his unusual response to the bush, the book, and the poetry—to quit reading his autobiography, because in a sense the central story of his life is about nothing else. Lewis's Joy is unsatisfied desire which is better than any satisfaction. This Joy has the stab and pang of longing.

When he was a young teenager, Lewis thought naturally enough that Joy was pointing him toward sex; but he learned that sex had nothing to do with it. They are separate things. He also learned that the lure of magic and the occult had nothing to do with it.

Lewis forgot about Joy for a while, but then he came across Arthur Rackham's illustrations for *Siegfried and the Twilight of the Gods*. Once again he was flooded with an unendurable sense of desire, and now he realized that this experience was what he valued most in life.

In April 1914 Lewis met Arthur Greeves, a neighbor boy outside Belfast, and he was amazed to learn that Arthur shared his passion for Norse mythology. Lewis later wrote, "I had been so far from thinking such a friend possible that I had never even longed for one; no more than I longed to be King of England."[3] Arthur too knew the stab of Joy. Now Lewis had someone to consult and to confide in. They shared their unusual love of natural beauty and their enthusiasm for certain art and literature.

A few months after meeting Arthur, Lewis hatched the idea of writing an allegory in which the stern, ugly, money-grubbing spirit would finally be conquered by that of art and

3. Ibid., chap. 8, p. 131.

beauty. "However," he admitted in his letter to Arthur, "this is only a castle in the air."[4] He didn't write the allegory.

As time went on and Lewis became an expert in Norse mythology, the thrill disappeared from it. Then once when Lewis was remembering a particularly vivid moment of his past Joy and was longing for it, he was stabbed by Joy again. Not Joy in Norse mythology, but Joy in his own past Joy in Norse mythology. As he put it, the very moment when he longed to be so stabbed again was itself such a stabbing.

When Lewis's attention was focused on his inner feelings, the Joy never came. When Northernness no longer produced Joy, he should have realized that the object of his desire was further away and more outside himself than Norse mythology, as he later admitted. He did not in fact realize that for a long time. He kept seeking the special sensation in every walk he took, in every poem he read.

Then in March 1916 Lewis came across the book *Phantastes* by George MacDonald, and although he did not realize it until later, Joy started to take on a holy quality for him. As he put it later, his imagination was baptized; in 1962 he listed this book as the one that had influenced him more than any other. Not that he got on the right track very soon. That came more than ten years later. Nevertheless, in a March 1916 letter to Arthur Greeves announcing his discovery of MacDonald, he observed lightly, "Perhaps one of these days you may even make a Christian of me."[5]

In July Lewis said he was sorry that Greeves disapproved

---

4. Lewis to Greeves, 20 October 1914, *They Stand Together: The Letters of C. S. Lewis to Arthur Greeves (1914–1963)*, ed. Walter Hooper (New York: Macmillan, 1979), 57.
5. Lewis to Greeves, 7 March 1916, *They Stand Together*, 93.

of his sneering remarks about Christianity as represented by characters in a story he was writing.[6] He assured Greeves that he was not sneering at Christianity itself. Three months later, however, Lewis dashed any hopes Greeves might have had that Lewis was open to Christianity.

In October Lewis lectured Greeves about "the recognised scientific account of the growth of religions."

> [Y]ou know, I think, that I believe in no religion. There is absolutely no proof for any of them, and from a philosophical standpoint Christianity is not even the best. All religions, that is, all mythologies to give them their proper name are merely man's own invention—Christ as much as Loki. Primitive man found himself surrounded by all sorts of terrible things he didn't understand....
>
> Thus religion, that is to say mythology grew up. Often, too, great men were regarded as gods after their death—such as Heracles or Odin: thus after the death of a Hebrew philosopher Yeshua (whose name we have corrupted into Jesus) he became regarded as a god, a cult sprang up, which was afterwards connected with the ancient Hebrew Jahweh-worship, and so Christianity came into being—one mythology among many....
>
> Of course, mind you, I am not laying down as a certainty that there *is* nothing outside the material world: considering the discoveries that are always being made, this would be foolish. Anything MAY exist.[7]

Lewis said he was sorry that Greeves was not free of Christianity, but he didn't feel that this difference between them was of much importance. He called the subject dry bones.

---

6. Lewis to Greeves, 18 July 1916, *They Stand Together*, 124.
7. Lewis to Greeves, 12 October 1916, *They Stand Together*, 135.

Just before he was sent to the trenches in France, Lewis wrote to Greeves that he had now discovered philosophy and metaphysics, which make other questions seem irrelevant. He advised Greeves to probe these matters in order to avoid the mental stagnation usually inherent in religious satisfaction.[8]

Six months later, recuperating from his war wounds, Lewis wrote to Greeves that he had changed his old views. A conviction was growing in him that spirit exists and that we come in contact with it through our aesthetic thrills. Through our inner sensations, beauty calls our spiritual nature away from time and space to "Something" superior to the material world.[9]

In 1919 Lewis published his first book of poetry, *Spirits in Bondage*. He said the main theme was that nature is wholly diabolical and malevolent and that God, if He exists, is outside and in opposition to the cosmic arrangement. He had expressed this view a year earlier in a letter to Greeves in the most compressed form possible: "Matter=Nature=Satan."[10]

The poem in *Spirits in Bondage* titled "Our Daily Bread" vividly expresses ideas that would appear later in mature form in *Pilgrim's Regress*. In the last three stanzas Lewis claimed that often in ordinary places he would suddenly hear a Living voice call to him or he would catch a glimpse of lands beyond the wall or see the face of a god. Someday, he predicted, this experience would force him to leave home and become a pilgrim, wandering in foreign places. He would seek the end of the world where he could cast himself into a sea of light that his spirit came from in the first place.[11]

8. Lewis to Greeves, 4 November 1917, *They Stand Together*, 202.
9. Lewis to Greeves, 29 May 1918, *They Stand Together*, 217.
10. Lewis to Greeves, 23 May 1918, *They Stand Together*, 214.
11. C. S. Lewis, *Spirits in Bondage: A Cycle of Lyrics,* ed. Walter Hooper (San Diego: Harcourt Brace Jovanovich, Harvest, 1984), 60.

*Spirits in Bondage* also includes a poem called "Song of the Pilgrims," in which seekers for truth express their discouragement because their search for the promised land takes so long. But they are sure that the land they seek is waiting for them and is worth all their hardships.[12] The final poem is about an island in the West. Speaking as a soldier dying on the battlefield in World War I, Lewis exclaims, "O Country of Dreams!" and contrasts the pain and brutality of war with the peaceful castle and dewy upland places in the garden of God where he hopes to be received. "Open the gates for me!" the soldier begs. But the soldier wants to be all alone in that beautiful place, dim and silent. The title of the poem makes no promise; it is simply "Death in Battle."[13] One can read this as more than a war poem; Lewis was writing about all human life.

So long as Lewis believed that his experience of Joy had all along been mainly a keen appreciation of beauty, he talked about its value a great deal and experienced it very little. He also wrote about it. In 1922, he noted in his journal that he had an abominable prose style and that between writing poetry and working he would probably never have time to improve it. He then wrote a poem titled "Joy." A couple of years later, when he began teaching philosophy at University College, it was published.[14]

By this time Lewis had been forced into a belief called Absolute Idealism. In this system the Absolute was a spirit much like God; but there was nothing to fear and nothing to

---

12. Ibid., 47–49.
13. Ibid., 74–75.
14. C. S. Lewis [Clive Hamilton, pseud.], "Joy," *The Beacon* 3, no. 31 (May 1924): 444–45. See also *Collected Poems of C. S. Lewis,* ed. Walter Hooper (London: Harper Collins, 1994), 243–44.

obey. The Absolute was safely impersonal.

In his slow vacillations about Joy, Lewis wrote a book-length poem more or less denouncing Joy. *Dymer,* which was begun in 1922 and published in 1926, traces the strange adventures of a young man who was born in "The Perfect City" but rebelled and left. This is in a sense the opposite of Bunyan's *Pilgrim's Progress,* in which the pilgrim was born in the City of Destruction but rebelled and left. Like *Pilgrim's Progress, Dymer* is an allegory. Dymer represents a man escaping from illusion, particularly the illusion of Joy. At the end of the story he is killed by a monster. In the preface to the 1950 edition, which Lewis called the exhumation of a dead book, he explained some aspects of the rather bitter allegory and described the mythlike basis of the book.

Lewis did not reject Joy for very long; instead, he developed a better perception of what it is. He finally realized that all sources of Joy are in essence reminders of something else; he did not know what. And he came to realize that Joy itself was a longing for something outside himself and his own experience. Finally Lewis decided that what he really wanted in his moments of clearest consciousness was to merge with the Absolute. It seems as if he had predicted this decision in his youthful poem "Our Daily Bread" when he claimed that someday he would become a pilgrim seeking the sea of light that was his origin, hoping to cast himself into it.[15]

One day, on a bus ride up Headington Hill outside Oxford, Lewis became aware that he was in some sense holding a door shut and that he could open it if he chose. He chose to open it, for whatever that meant. For the rest of his

---

15. Lewis, *Spirits in Bondage,* 60.

life he laid great stress on choice and will. After the decision in the bus, Lewis's philosophical defenses against the existence of a personal God began to crumble. His account of his final surrender to this personal God, as he described it in the climax of his autobiography, has become famous: "In the Trinity Term of 1929 I gave in, and admitted that God was God, and knelt and prayed: perhaps, that night, the most dejected and reluctant convert in all England."[16]

After this conversion to theism Lewis began to attend church and to read the Bible daily, although he was not yet a believing Christian. For the first time he found the element of Christianity in *Pilgrim's Progress* likable. Lewis did not announce his change of position to many people. He wrote to his friend Owen Barfield, "Terrible things are happening to me. The 'Spirit' or 'Real I' is showing an alarming tendency to become much more personal and is taking the offensive, and behaving just like God. You'd better come on Monday at the latest or I may have entered a monastery."[17] He wrote to Arthur Greeves in 1930 about the beauty of finding himself "on the main road with all humanity," referring to his belief in God.[18] (Almost three years later he would be using "the main road" as a key image in *Pilgrim's Regress*.) To his friend A. K. Hamilton-Jenkin, Lewis wrote, "It is not precisely Christianity, though it may turn out that way in the end."[19]

At this time Lewis was reading some Christian books,

---

16. Lewis, *Surprised by Joy,* chap. 14, 228–29.
17. Lewis to Barfield, 1930, *Letters of C. S. Lewis*, edited and with a memoir by W. H. Lewis, revised and enlarged edition edited by Walter Hooper (San Diego: Harcourt, Brace & Co., Harvest, 1993), 283–84.
18. Lewis to Greeves, 26 January 1930, *They Stand Together,* 333–34.
19. Lewis to Hamilton-Jenkin, 21 March 1930, Marion E. Wade Center, Wheaton College, Wheaton, Ill.

including two MacDonald fantasies for children that gave him spiritual insights. These were *The Princess and the Goblin* and *The Princess and Curdie*. Sometime during this pre-Christian period, Lewis began a factual prose precursor to *Pilgrim's Regress* telling about his conversion. According to Lewis literary-estate manager Walter Hooper, the sixty-five-year-old, seventy-two-page manuscript begins, "In this book I propose to describe the process by which I came back, like so many of my generation, from materialism to a belief in God."[20] This essay is not available to researchers.

From the age of sixteen onwards Lewis's one main aim in life had been to become a successful author. Now, fifteen years later, he felt that he was an unmistakable failure. In a memorable letter written to Arthur Greeves in mid-1930, he said he believed this was a blessing. Writing does a person no harm, but the ambition to be distinguished above others for one's writing is counter to the nature of the Kingdom of God. Literary success is, in the long run, dust and ashes. Lewis urged Greeves, who also yearned to be an author, to think of the spiritual cost for a person who succeeded as a writer.[21] Exactly two years later Lewis would be with Greeves, writing *Pilgrim's Regress* at a prodigious pace.

In the same letter, Lewis told Greeves that he had much higher standards for the religious poems he was working on that summer than he had ever had for his writing when he did it in hopes of publication. Lewis had copied nine of these

---

20. Roger Lancelyn Green and Walter Hooper, *C. S. Lewis: A Biography*, rev. ed. (San Diego: Harcourt, Brace & Co., Harvest, 1994), 112–13. There is no doubt Lewis wrote a prose precursor (see *They Stand Together*, 378–81). The question is whether it still exists or not. Hooper did not store it with his other Lewis manuscripts in the Bodleian Library, and he has not yet published it.
21. Lewis to Greeves, 18 August 1930, *They Stand Together*, 378–81.

poems into a little booklet which he titled "Half Hours with Hamilton, or Quiet Moments." Clive Hamilton was the pen name he used until he wrote *Pilgrim's Regress,* which he signed with his own name. He prefaced the nine poems with an amusing bit of banter and gave the set to his friend Owen Barfield; but the poems are serious. Two years later Lewis would incorporate these nine poems into *Pilgrim's Regress.*

Near the end of 1931, Lewis had Bunyan's *Pilgrim's Progress* in mind and mentioned how much he liked some of the words in it. (Eight years later he wrote to his brother about being a Christian: "How on earth did we manage to enjoy all these books so much as we did in the days when we had really no conception of what was at the centre of them?")[22] On the evening of September 19 in 1931 Lewis had his friends Hugo Dyson and J. R. R. Tolkien to dinner at Magdalen College, and then the three walked about the college grounds and talked in Lewis's rooms for hours. Their walking was interrupted at one point by a very peculiar rush of night wind which gave Lewis a feeling of ecstasy. Tolkien stayed until 3:00 A.M. and Dyson stayed until 4:00 A.M., discussing Christianity in depth.

Shortly after that memorable evening, Lewis wrote to Arthur Greeves and told him about it. In this letter he told Greeves that the books by William Morris filled him with desire for hauntingly beautiful lands that always fail to satisfy —which drives one on toward the real thing. According to Lewis, Morris shows a person just how far one can go without knowing God, and by then a person is forced to go further, although Morris failed to do so. The Christian conception of

---

22. C. S. Lewis to W. H. Lewis, 18 December 1939, *Letters of C. S. Lewis,* 331.

death, Lewis decided, is the answer to Morris's search for a beautiful paradise.[23]

Nine days later, Lewis mentioned in the middle of a long letter to Arthur Greeves, "I have just passed on from believing in God to definitely believing in Christ—in Christianity. I will try to explain this another time. My long night talk with Dyson and Tolkien had a good deal to do with it."[24] Then he went on chatting about some poets and about the work that he and his brother were doing in the woods on their property, as if the news of his conversion was a very minor matter.

On October 18 Lewis responded to questions from Greeves by saying that he had never before understood the miracle of Christ's redemption enough to accept it.[25] Once he saw that the Christian story could be perceived through imagination as the most important and meaningful of all myths, he began to understand it enough to really believe it as history and fact.

In January 1932 Lewis wrote to his brother that he had recently read *The Wood between the Worlds* by William Morris, and that he wished that Morris had written a hundred more books of that type.[26] Soon Lewis began a project that seemed to combine his pleasure in Morris's otherworldly locales, his love of narrative poetry, his fascination with allegory, his appreciation of *Pilgrim's Progress,* and his desire to explain his recent acceptance of Christianity. He decided to tell of an allegorical search for Joy that led him to his new faith. This story was to be a very long narrative poem about

---

23. Lewis to Greeves, 22 September 1931, *They Stand Together,* 421–22.
24. Lewis to Greeves, 1 October 1931, *They Stand Together,* 425.
25. Lewis to Greeves, 18 October 1931, *They Stand Together,* 426–28.
26. C. S. Lewis to W. H. Lewis, 17 January 1932, *Letters of C. S. Lewis,* 297.

an ocean voyage, written in hexameter like Homer's *Odyssey*.[27] Beginning with the lines "I will write down the portion that I understand / Of twenty years wherein I went from land to land," Lewis went on to claim that he went halfway round the world searching for a home.[28] He was driven away from every land until he finally submitted to making his home in the one land he feared, where he finally found security.

The unpublished second stanza is a prayer to God for nurture and guidance to enable Lewis to complete this book well for the sake of readers who might be helped by it. In this stanza he likens God to a self-enkindled flame and likens himself to a fading candle; he describes God as unquivering light and the warmth of the world. He feels too reverent to use the word God. In the third stanza, Lewis recalls that in his childhood he heard the Christian story, but it didn't interest him. He was much more interested in the joys of being alive in the world than in any news about his soul.[29]

Lewis was enthusiastic about the poem's beginning. In a letter to Owen Barfield, he said he was pleased with it and that the old epic structure was very useful in such a project, although Wordsworth had failed to see that fact.[30] Later he sent a sample to Barfield and received encouragement. Lewis responded, "It really takes a load off my mind to hear that you like the poem."[31] He added that although couplets are

---

27. Since Lewis's poem needs a title, I would suggest *Odyssey*.
28. Green and Hooper, *C. S. Lewis: A Biography*, 127.
29. Lewis to Barfield, 6 May 1932, Letters from C. S. Lewis to Owen Barfield, vol. 2 (1932–1940), cat. no. 26–50, index no. 0055–0097, Marion E. Wade Center, Wheaton College, Wheaton, Ill. This letter contains 34 lines of the long poem described above, the only remaining part of the poem. Managers of the C. S. Lewis literary estate did not grant permission to publish this 34-line poem here. It is available only at the Wade Center and the Bodleian Library.
30. Lewis to Barfield, 19 March 1932, Letters from C. S. Lewis to Owen Barfield.
31. Lewis to Barfield, 6 May 1932, Letters from C. S. Lewis to Owen Barfield.

dangerous for such a purpose, he needed them to add swing and zest to his story in the old epic style. He admitted that such an autobiographical poem was ludicrously ambitious, but he expected to continue working on it for several years before giving up. Less than six months later, in a letter to Barfield, Lewis declared the poem a failure in itself, but observed that it had been part of the preparation for what happened to him next.[32]

Although Lewis never really traveled far by sea, he had frequently traveled by sea between England and his old home in Ireland for over twenty years. Now his father was dead and his old home was no longer available. He was very tired in August of 1932 and asked his friend Arthur Greeves if he could come over to visit him for a two-week vacation. It was a fateful two weeks. Between August 15 and August 29, *Pilgrim's Regress* "spurted out so suddenly," in Lewis's own words.[33]

Greeves made three suggestions for improvement of the book which Lewis did not follow. Greeves suggested leaving out all the Greek and Latin quotations, and Lewis answered that we need more classical learning, not less. Greeves suggested that Lewis should use a more formal and dignified style of writing; Lewis answered that he intended to be idiomatic and racy. Greeves would have preferred a simpler book with less complicated meanings, and Lewis answered that his conversion had not been simple and so the book could not be simple.[34]

Twenty years later Lewis might have thought that Greeves

---

32. Lewis to Barfield, 29 October 1932, Letters from C. S. Lewis to Owen Barfield.
33. Lewis to Owen Barfield, 29 October 1932, excerpt quoted in Green and Hooper, *C. S. Lewis: A Biography*, 128.
34. Lewis to Greeves, 4 December 1932, *They Stand Together*, 444–45.

was correct about readability, because in a personal letter to a confused reader named Mrs. Edward Allen he said he wasn't surprised that she had trouble with *Pilgrim's Regress*. He explained that it had been his first religious book and that he did not then know how to write an easy book. Furthermore, he had not really tried to make the book easy because he never dreamed that he would have any readers outside a small "highbrow" circle.[35] Greeves might have enjoyed that admission.

Many readers of *Pilgrim's Regress* realize that Lewis was copying John Bunyan's *Pilgrim's Progress* when he set his story in a dream. But relatively few readers realize that this popular narrative device was widely employed by great medieval poets. In these visionary allegories, the narrator falls asleep and, while sleeping, dreams the events which are related. Often a guide leads the narrator. Allegory plays a significant role in the events.[36] Medieval visionary allegories include the thirteenth-century *Romance of the Rose,* Dante's *Divine Comedy,* Langland's *Piers Plowman,* and numerous dream poems of Chaucer such as *Parliament of Fowls, The House of Fame,* and the *Book of the Duchess.*[37] Lewis later returned to the dream narrative in *The Great Divorce* (1945), which among his own books was one of his personal favorites.

By the end of 1932 Lewis had finished polishing the manu-

---

35. Lewis to Allen, 19 January 1953, *Letters of C. S. Lewis,* 430.
36. M. H. Abrams, *A Glossary of Literary Terms,* 3rd ed. (New York: Holt, Rinehart, & Winston, 1974), s.v. "dream vision." See also C. S. Lewis, *Allegory of Love: A Study in Medieval Tradition* (New York: Oxford University Press, 1936) for a discussion of the medieval allegorical method.
37. See Lewis's *Discarded Image: An Introduction to Medieval and Renaissance Literature* (Cambridge: Cambridge University Press, 1964), 60–65, for a discussion of the "feignedsomnia" of allegorical dream-poems of the Middle Ages. The *somnium* "shows us truths veiled in an allegorical form." (p. 63). See also Kathryn Lindskoog, *The Gift of Dreams: A Christian View* (San Francisco: Harper & Row, 1979).

script, prepared a fanciful map, and found a publisher—J. M. Dent. At that point Lewis dedicated the book to Arthur Greeves and told him in a letter, "It is yours by every right—written in your house, read to you as it was written, and celebrating . . . an experience which I have more in common with you than anyone else."[38]

Lewis refused to allow Dent to include illustrations, but Dent forced Lewis to shorten the book's original title, *The Pilgrim's Regress, or Pseudo-Bunyan's Periplus: An Allegorical Apology for Christianity, Reason and Romanticism.* Because *periplus*, which means circumnavigation, is an obscure word and this title is unwieldy, they cut it down to its present form. Ten years later Lewis was to regret his use of the word Romanticism in the title because it did not convey the meaning he intended.

(Lewis's meaning is not lost on everyone. Sixty years after publication of *The Pilgrim's Regress: An Allegorical Apology for Christianity, Reason, and Romanticism,* Dr. Fraser Watts, inaugural professor of the controversial Starbridge Lectureship in Science and Theology at Cambridge University, stated that Western thought has been shaped by three broad traditions: Judeo-Christian, the Enlightenment/Rationalist, and the Romantic.)[39]

One thousand copies were printed in May 1933, but they did not sell well. Lewis found that his six gift copies were gone before he knew it, and so he had to buy a copy to give to Arthur Greeves in June. "I think it is going to be at least as big a failure as *Dymer*," he observed wryly, but he claimed that he

---

38. Lewis to Greeves, 25 March 1933, *They Stand Together,* 452.
39. Linda Joffee, "Bridging the Science-Religion Divide," *Christian Science Monitor,* 27 July 1994, 12.

was accepting the disappointment fairly well.[40] A review in the *Times Literary Supplement* referred to Lewis's poetic gift that "pulls the reader up in the midst of the smooth-flowing narrative to admire its energy and profundity."[41]

In 1935 the book was accepted by Sheed and Ward, a Roman Catholic company that increased its sales. However, Lewis was extremely unhappy with two comments that this company placed on the flyleaf of the dust jacket: "Mr. Lewis's wit would probably seem to Bunyan sinful. Certainly his theology would. . . . The hero, brought up in Puritania (Mr. Lewis himself was born in Ulster), cannot abide the religion he finds there." The latter is an indictment of the Anglican Protestantism of Northern Ireland. Lewis wrote in the flyleaf of the copy he gave his father, "The suggestions are put in by the unspeakable Sheed with no authority of mine & without my knowledge."[42]

A reviewer in the *New York Times Book Review* referred to *Pilgrim's Regress* as "a modern man's intricate journey through the worlds of thought and feeling and desire; his passionate search for truth . . . a picture of genuine mystical experience, rationalized by philosophy. . . . To many it will seem like a fresh wind blowing across arid wastes."[43] (On the back of the 1992 edition of *The Pilgrim's Regress* the passage is slightly misquoted, ending with "To many it will seem like a fresh wind blowing across arid waters.") A review in the

---

40. Lewis to Greeves, 13 June 1933, *They Stand Together*, 454.
41. *Times Literary Supplement*, 6 July 1933, 456.
42. This copy of the book, with Lewis's angry comment, may be seen in the Wade Center at Wheaton College in Wheaton, Illinois. For a delightful and understanding filial tribute to "the unspeakable Sheed," read "Frank Sheed and Maisie Ward: Writers, Publishers, and Parents" in *The Good Word*, by their son Wilfrid Sheed (Dutton, 1978).
43. J. S. Southron, *New York Times Book Review*, 8 December 1935, 7.

*Catholic World* declared, "This brilliantly written volume is a caustic, devastating critique of modern philosophy, religion, politics and art; a clear-cut, logical and effective apologia of reason and the Christian faith. . . . We have rarely read a book we so thoroughly enjoyed. We are convinced that the author too enjoyed the writing of every line."[44]

Lewis offered to send a gift copy to his friend Sister Penelope, who lived in an English convent, "if I can get one out of my publisher—who is a difficult man."[45] On the last day of 1939 Lewis wrote to his brother that his friend Mary Neylan, an ex-pupil, was a gratifyingly constant rereader of the *Regress*. He hoped she might become a Christian.[46] (Indeed, Mrs. Neylan became a Christian, as Lewis hoped.) The story in *Pilgrim's Regress* is one he always liked to share.

In 1943 Lewis added a helpful nine-page preface and running headlines for his book's third publisher, Geoffrey Bles. Most readers are dependent upon these helps, and Greeves would have appreciated them. But others enjoy the challenge of trying to understand the book as first published. Erik Routley, an undergraduate of Magdalen, Lewis's college, had fond memories of sitting up with friends who shared his lodgings at Oxford and wrestling with the meanings and allegorical references unaided. They were pleased to see later in the preface and headlines that their hard-won interpretations were mainly correct.[47]

---

44. The Reverend Bertrand Conway, *Catholic World,* May 1936.
45. Lewis to Sister Penelope, 24 August 1939, C. S. Lewis Letters to Sister Penelope, vol. 1 (1939–1948), cat. no. 1–35, index no. 0001–0057, Marion E. Wade Center, Wheaton College, Wheaton, Ill.
46. C. S. Lewis to Warren H. Lewis, 31 December 1939, C. S. Lewis Letters to Warren H. Lewis, vol. 4 (31 December 1939–15 February 1940), index no. 0113–0148, Marion E. Wade Center, Wheaton College, Wheaton, Ill.
47. Erik Routley, "A Prophet," in *C. S. Lewis at the Breakfast Table and Other Reminiscences,* ed. James T. Como (New York: Macmillan, 1979), 36.

Although Routley and many others have highly recommended *Pilgrim's Regress,* there is a widespread rumor that Lewis later regretted the book. I first encountered that idea in 1969 in Peter Kreeft's booklet *C. S. Lewis: A Critical Essay:* "*Pilgrim's Regress,* an obscure and uncharitable post-conversion manifesto, which Lewis accurately labels his worst book...."[48]

In 1974 I encountered an echo of Kreeft's idea in an unsuccessful thesis titled "Five Main Theological Themes in the Fiction of C. S. Lewis." The thesis explained blithely: "I excluded *The Pilgrim's Regress* because an adequate treatment of its philosophical contents would surpass its merits. (It was Lewis' worst book as he himself admits.)" Years later I heard the same error repeated with seeming authority by an influential American editor of various books by and about Lewis.

The original source of this error may be a misreading of the following statement Lewis made eight years after he added his 1943 preface and running headlines: "The only printed verse of mine outside the *Regress* (and a *very* early volume wh. I don't want remembered) is a poem called Dymer."[49] If a reader skips the word *and,* it seems that Lewis is wishing *Pilgrim's Regress* would be forgotten. But a correct reading makes it clear that Lewis was disowning only his first book, *Spirits in Bondage.*

In 1954 Lewis wrote to Alan Bede Griffiths about his longing for heaven: "All joy (as distinct from mere pleasure, still more amusement) emphasises our pilgrim status: always reminds, beckons, awakens desire. Our best havings are want-

---

48. Peter Kreeft, *C. S. Lewis: A Critical Essay* (Grand Rapids, Mich.: William B. Eerdmans Publishing, 1969), 6.
49. Lewis to William Kinter, 14 January 1951, C. S. Lewis Letters to Miscellaneous Correspondents, index no. 727–771D, Marion E. Wade Center, Wheaton College, Wheaton, Ill.

ings."[50] Bede Griffiths had been a student of Lewis's when Lewis was becoming a theist, and was a friend of Lewis's when Lewis became a Christian. Griffiths had become a Christian then also, and later became a Benedictine monk serving in India. In 1955 Lewis retold the story of *Pilgrim's Regress* in his straightforward account of his life pilgrimage, *Surprised by Joy*. He dedicated *Surprised by Joy* to his old friend and fellow pilgrim Bede Griffiths.[51]

In 1958 Eerdmans duplicated the Bles edition of *Pilgrim's Regress* in a paperback edition in the United States. Eerdmans used the Bles cover design of an armored knight on a black horse, but added a plume to the helmet and gave the knight an egg-shaped face. (In the story it was Reason, not John, who wore the armor and rode the horse.) Four years after Eerdmans published the first American edition of *Pilgrim's Regress*, Lewis completed his earthly pilgrimage.

In 1981 a fifth publisher, Bantam, issued *Pilgrim's Regress* without Lewis's headlines; and Eerdmans issued a deluxe edition illustrated by Michael Hague, which was reissued as a paperback in 1992. Michael Hague dressed the characters in costumes appropriate for John Bunyan's day. The illustrated edition includes Lewis's headlines and presents Lewis's 1943 preface as an afterword.

*Pilgrim's Regress* was Lewis's first Christian book, his first prose book, the apparent seedbed of many of the ideas he developed later, and his only prose allegory. But we will never quite understand how John's journey came to be written in two weeks. Lewis indicated to his friend Owen Barfield that

---

50. Lewis to Dom Bede Griffiths, 5 November 1954, *Letters of C. S. Lewis*, 441.
51. For Alan Bede Griffiths' account of his conversion and Lewis's, see Griffiths' essay "The Adventure of Faith" in *C. S. Lewis at the Breakfast Table*, 11-24.

his first two attempts—a prose account of his conversion to theism, and then a verse account of his conversion to Christianity—had evidently primed the pump.[52] The only other hint Lewis left us was in an address called "The Vision of John Bunyan" that he wrote in 1962 and read on BBC Radio, thirty years after he wrote *Pilgrim's Regress*.[53]

Lewis explains that it is often futile to ask how a great book came into existence. But Bunyan has told us the answer in his own case, so far as such things can be told. He says that while he was at work on quite a different book he "fell suddenly into an Allegory."[54] Lewis takes this to mean that Bunyan thought of a little allegory that would have filled a single paragraph. But Bunyan wrote down twenty things, only to find that twenty more had come into his head. They "began *'to multiply'* like sparks flying out of a fire."[55] These ideas couldn't be contained in the book he had been working on; they insisted on splitting off from it and becoming a new book. Bunyan went along with the process. Lewis especially liked Bunyan's description of what Lewis himself calls golden moments of unimpeded composition: "Still as I pull'd, it came."[56] Bunyan was saying that once he had caught hold of the method for writing *Pilgrim's Progress*, he just kept pulling and the phrases kept coming.

*"It came,"* Lewis exclaims, echoing Bunyan. "I doubt if we shall ever know more of the process called 'inspiration' than

---

52. Lewis to Barfield, 19 March 1932, 6 May 1932, 29 October 1932, Letters from C. S. Lewis to Owen Barfield.
53. C. S. Lewis, "The Vision of John Bunyan," in *Selected Literary Essays*, ed. Walter Hooper (Cambridge: Cambridge University Press, 1969), xix, 146–153.
54. John Bunyan, "Author's Apology for His Book," in *The Pilgrim's Progress* (New York: Lancer Books, Magnum Easy Eye Books, 1968), 7.
55. Lewis, "Vision of John Bunyan," 147.
56. Bunyan, "Author's Apology," 8.

those two monosyllables tell us."[57] That is, perhaps, the most that can be said about the torrent of creativity that produced *Pilgrim's Regress* between August 15 and August 29 in 1932. Lewis pull'd, and it came.

---

57. Lewis, "Vision of John Bunyan," 147.

BOOK ONE

# THE DATA

## John's Predicament

Book 1 of *Pilgrim's Regress*, "The Data," consists of six chapters. It begins with Lewis's simple statement that he, as the writer, dreamed this story of John in his sleep. Book 1 ends with John stealing away from home while his parents sleep. The sleep and dream motif—Lewis was a vivid dreamer all his life—occurs throughout *Pilgrim's Regress*.

Book 1 traces John's story from his birth to his setting out on his quest. It is told with an immediacy similar to that in the Gospel of Mark. Like the first few chapters of Genesis, the first few chapters of *Pilgrim's Regress* are easy to read but call for especially close attention. They are both emotionally evocative and ironic. Book 1 is dreamlike, with a run-on quality; but it is also spare and compact. Time seems compressed.

The characters in book 1 include John, his parents, the cook, the Steward, Uncle George, the brown girl and her offspring, and the mysterious man in the coach. Key objects in book 1 include John's parents' garden, the woods, primroses, the road, a bird and a sling, masks, a rule card, a black hole, a stone religious building, a stone wall with a window, and an Island.

John's predicament, the subject of book 1, consists of (1) moral failure, (2) fear of the Landlord, and (3) desire for Joy.

# 1

## THE RULES

### *John's Early Religious Training*

Here begins the story of a pilgrim named John. Why John? First, in our culture the name John stands for Everyman. It is said that at one time over half the men in England were named John. Second, John was the name of the author of *Pilgrim's Progress,* and so it is the name that is most readily associated with a pilgrim. Third, C. S. Lewis was "Jack" to friends and relatives ever since he was four years old and suddenly decided to answer only to Jacksie.[1] Jack, of course, is a nickname for John. So Lewis himself spent his personal life responding to the nickname for John. Fourth, and surely most important, the meaning of the original Hebrew form of the name John is "God has been gracious."

The careful reader soon notices an inordinate number of *and*s in the first paragraph of this story. There are twenty-four *and*s on the first brief page. This stylization gives the beginning narrative a childlike quality and a sense of urgency. If it were not for the break caused by John's staccato conversation with the cook, the entire chapter would probably be one unbroken paragraph.

---

1. W. H. Lewis, "Memoir of C. S. Lewis," in *Letters of C. S. Lewis,* ed. Walter Hooper (San Diego: Harcourt, Brace & Co., Harvest, 1993), 22.

John's first action in *Pilgrim's Regress* is leaving home in the second sentence. The entire story is to be about his heading away from and back to his home and his Home. One of the earliest recorded statements of C. S. Lewis himself, when he was only twenty-one months old, was "Not going home."[2] That was what he kept insisting when he was on holiday with his mother and brother in Ballycastle and the end of their delightful vacation was approaching.

If one is to guess at John's age when he plunged after pleasure in the woods and was smacked by his mother, two years is most likely. John was going after primroses, and in the language of flowers primroses symbolize youth. In the story a year passed in only five words. John was probably three when he took aim at a bird in the garden and got smacked by the cook. There is a great change. When John was smacked at two he simply wept. But when he was smacked at three he held back his tears and started to ask questions instead. In psychological jargon, he moved from the emotive to the cognitive response.

John's earliest questions were Why? Who is the Steward? Why? Who is the Landlord? Why? His mother spent an entire afternoon explaining the answers. That was his punishment for asking. At two John had been too young to ask questions; at three he was too young to take in the answers.

Again in the story a year passed in only five words. The rest of chapter 1 describes John's first formal religious training. The day was, of course, dismal. The clothes were, of course, ugly and itchy. John's parents first escorted him too solicitously,

---

[2]. Flora Lewis to Albert Lewis, Lewis Papers: Memoirs of the Lewis Family 1850–1930, ed. by W. H. Lewis, Marion E. Wade Center, Wheaton College, Wheaton, Ill., vol. 2, p. 310.

then threatened him about the Steward's anger, then temporarily deserted him. At this point John began to be afraid.

John's fear was increased by the Steward's mask, his list of overwhelming rules, the necessity of lying to the Steward about the rules, and the information that if John broke any of the rules the Landlord would shut him up forever in a black hole full of snakes and scorpions. John did not cry in his new distress. He asked a question instead. He asked without tears whether anything could save him from the snakes and lobsters—in his consternation he forgot about the scorpions—if by chance he ever broke one little rule. The answer from the Steward was incomprehensible.

The unpredictable changes in demeanor and mixed messages of the Steward are just the kind of contradictions that produce anxiety in children. So John's fear was compounded. The instruction that John received from his mother and the Steward seemed to do him nothing but harm.

## 2

### THE ISLAND

### *Called to a Glimpse of Joy*

Lewis reminds us that he is still dreaming and that John is still a young child. The entire chapter is one unbroken paragraph, although it is about two opposite subjects—fear and Joy. John had discovered some contradictory rules on the back of his rule card from the Steward. But for weeks he was obsessed with his inability to keep all the rules on the front of the rule card and tortured by his fear of the black hole. "The other Law in his members" mentioned in the headline is a reference to man's predisposition to sin as described in Romans 7:22–23.

For the third time in the story John went out onto the road. The first time, he crossed it just to explore, discovered a beautiful wood, and was smacked for punishment. The second time, he was taken along the road to the dark stone house of the Steward. The third time, he entered the road in an attempt to escape his fear. This time he encountered a musical sound, a voice that said Come, and a stone wall with a window in it. What he saw through the window reminded him of his first discovery of woodland beauty, and then he had his first experience of Joy. It temporarily shattered his worldview; his fear lifted, he asked no questions, and he wept. Weeping is always important in John's story. It happens at rare moments of special grace when John's ego defenses against guilt and fear (his struggle for control and autonomy) dissolve; then for a second he is like an innocent, vulnerable child again, free of pride and in touch with spiritual reality.

Twenty years after writing this passage, Lewis described a similarly unforgettable numinous experience in *The Voyage of the "Dawn Treader"*: "And suddenly there came a breeze from the east.... It lasted only a second or so but what it brought them in that second none of those three children will ever forget. It brought both a smell and a sound, a musical sound. Edmund and Eustace would never talk about it afterward. Lucy could only say, 'It would break your heart.' 'Why,' said I, 'was it so sad?' 'Sad! No,' said Lucy."[3]

At first John knew that "seeing an Island" was only an approximation of his experience. But as he had tried in baby-

---

3. C. S. Lewis, *The Voyage of the "Dawn Treader"* (New York: Macmillan, 1952), chap. 16, p. 206.

hood to pull up primroses by the handfuls, now he seized greedily the idea of a magic Island. (The Oreads mentioned in the description were mountain nymphs.) He falsely convinced himself that he knew what he was after.

3

THE EASTERN MOUNTAINS

*Encounter with Death*

When John's uncle received an unexpected eviction notice from the Landlord, he nodded agreement with the Steward that all would surely be well—because he was too terrified to speak. The others, including John, put on masks to cover their fear, but Uncle George was trembling too violently to wear a mask, and his gray face became dreadful to behold. Over twenty years later, in *Till We Have Faces,* Lewis described how another man spoke bravely and calmly about his impending death, but the shaking of his body betrayed his fear to a concerned child.[4]

For the fourth time John went out on the road, walking East with his family into growing chill and gloom. At the brook Uncle George found his voice, but by then it was only the voice of a frightened child. He crossed the brook alone and walked away toward the Landlord's cold, black eastern mountain, never to be seen again. As Vertue says at the end of *Pilgrim's Regress,* "Something is being ended. It is a real brook."[5]

In the sad and horrifying experience of his uncle's death, John did not cry. He returned to asking questions instead.

---

4. C. S. Lewis, *Till We Have Faces* (New York: Harcourt, Brace & Co., 1957), chap. 2, pp. 17–18.
5. *The Pilgrim's Regress*, deluxe illustrated edition (Grand Rapids, Mich.: William B. Eerdmans Publishing, 1981), book 10, chap. 10, p. 197.

Again the answers were all confusing and contradictory.

In 1908, when Lewis was nine, he was suddenly bereaved three times. His uncle died, his grandfather who shared the Lewis home died, and his mother died slowly from extremely painful cancer. In the terms of *Pilgrim's Regress*, nobody ever saw them again.

The year 1908 is connected with *Pilgrim's Regress* in a way other than being the year when death struck the child Lewis. In 1908 G. K. Chesterton published his Christian classic *Orthodoxy*, and in 1918 Lewis started reading books by Chesterton. (In the June 6, 1962, issue of the *Christian Century*, Lewis listed Chesterton's *Everlasting Man* second of the ten books that had influenced him the most.) Because Chesterton began *Orthodoxy* with the merry tale of a muddled English yachtsman who discovered England under the impression that it was a new island in the South Seas, some think that Lewis basically combined *Orthodoxy* with *Pilgrim's Progress* when he created *Pilgrim's Regress*.[6]

Whether John is at heart the English yachtsman or not, a portion of Chesterton's preface fits *Pilgrim's Regress* very well.

> It is the purpose of the writer to attempt an explanation, not of whether the Christian Faith can be believed, but of how he personally has come to believe it. The book is therefore arranged upon the positive principle of a riddle and its answer. It deals first with all the writer's own solitary and sincere speculations and then with all the startling style in which they were all suddenly satisfied by the Christian Theology.[7]

---

6. Roger Lancelyn Green and Walter Hooper, *C. S. Lewis: A Biography,* rev. ed. (San Diego: Harcourt, Brace & Co., Harvest, 1994), 127.
7. G. K. Chesterton, preface to *Orthodoxy* (New York: Doubleday, 1959).

This passage, a suitable preface for *Pilgrim's Regress*, was published the very year when Lewis saw his mother, uncle, and grandfather disappear into the cold, dark land beyond the brook.

4

LEAH FOR RACHEL

*Lust as a Substitute for Joy*

Lewis turns from John's childhood to his boyhood and takes us deeper into the story when he says, "I turned over in my sleep and began to dream deeper still." He was dreaming us deeper into the difficult predicament, not deeper into the meaning of Joy. Unfortunately, John moved from yearning for the sight and sound of the Island to determining that he would explore the wood no matter what. Then for the first time he heard the music calling him up the road, and for the first time he decided not to follow the music. He preferred to insist upon finding the Island according to his own plan. (Perhaps the person he glimpsed on the road was the Man who was to help him later.)

One of the key sentences in the entire story is "[I]f I go a new way I shall not be able to insist: I shall just have to take what comes." John's will has gone wrong.

When his plan did not work, John came to believe that what he wanted from the Island was just a feeling. Then he found that he could not produce the feeling, because observing a feeling inhibits it. Lewis had read Samuel Alexander's *Space, Time and Deity* (first published in 1920) a few years before writing *Pilgrim's Regress* and was greatly impressed by

Alexander's differentiation between enjoyment of a mental experience and contemplation of the object of that experience, such as an Island. When one's attention moves from the object to the emotion itself, the process is short-circuited.

Lewis had read a vastly simpler presentation of that fact in his boyhood. His friend and biographer Roger Lancelyn Green has pointed out Lewis's lifelong delight in the stories of Edith Nesbit and the fact that as a child Lewis read "The Aunt and Amabel." This is Nesbit's story of an eight-year-old girl who entered a magic wardrobe in her great-aunt's spare bedroom, discovered a railway station there named "Bigwardrobeinspareroom," and took a train to the city of Whereyouwantogoto. (Lewis clearly echoed elements of this story in the opening chapters of *The Lion, the Witch and the Wardrobe,* in which a little girl entered a magic wardrobe and found herself in Narnia, where a faun thought she had come from the city of War Drobe in the land of Spare Oom.)[8]

Before her wonderful adventure, Amabel had been banished for hours to her aunt's spare bedroom as punishment. The large wardrobe there had a looking glass in it. "The first thing Amabel did was to look at herself in the glass. She was still sniffing and sobbing, and her eyes were swimming in tears, another one rolled down her nose as she looked—that was very interesting. Another rolled down, and that was the last, because as soon as you get interested in watching your tears they stop."[9]

Determined to experience something special, but unable to get what he wanted, John took the first substitute that came along. The title "Leah for Rachel" refers to the story in

---

8. Green and Hooper, *C. S. Lewis: A Biography,* 250–51.
9. Edith Nesbit, "The Aunt and Amabel," in *The Magic World* (1909; reprint, London: Ernest Benn, 1959; distributed in the U.S. by Putnam Publishing Group, Coward), 221.

Genesis 29 in which Jacob was tricked by his Uncle Laban into accepting Leah for his wife instead of her sister Rachel, whom he loved. John accepted lust instead of insisting upon Joy as he had intended to do. Roger Lancelyn Green, who discussed with Lewis the use that Lewis made of pictures that came into his sleeping or waking mind, suspected that the brown girl in *Pilgrim's Regress* originated in a vivid dream about a brown girl that Lewis recorded in his diary in 1922.[10]

## 5

### ICHABOD

### *Lust's Legacy*

Lewis had dreamed that John was in some sense asleep during his woodland relationship with the brown girl, and one cold day John awakened and realized that there was nothing here that he liked at all. Hence the title of the chapter, "Ichabod," meaning "the glory has departed." In 1 Samuel 4:21 a new mother named her baby son Ichabod because he was born right after a great tragedy: the ark of the covenant had been captured by the Philistines, the baby's father had been killed in battle, and his grandfather, Eli the priest, had died from the shock of the defeat.

The birth in this story is tragic in a different way and produces a host of temptations to bedevil John in the future.

---

10. Roger Lancelyn Green, "In the Evening," in *C. S. Lewis at the Breakfast Table and Other Reminiscences*, ed. James T. Como (New York: Macmillan, 1979), 213.

## 6

### QUEM QUAERITIS IN SEPULCHRO? NON EST HIC

*Recalled to Joy*

Now John's predicament was intensified because back home from the woods he found his guilt and fear worse than ever. He began to keep miserable vigils at the window in the broken stone wall, staring hopelessly into the bleak little wood. The source of the title "Quem Quaeritis in Sepulchro? Non Est Hic" is Luke 24:5–6 in the Latin Vulgate: "Whom do you seek in the sepulcher? He is not here." That was the message of the angels to the women who came to the tomb of Jesus with spices and found the stone rolled away and the body gone. John was staring into an empty grave also.

Then one night on the road when for once he was neither questioning, fearing, nor insisting, John broke down and wept. He longed for his lost longing. And at that point it came again. Again the music, the glimpse, the voice saying Come. This time John was willing to try the new way where he could not insist, where he would have to take what comes. This time John followed.

In book 1, John has learned the little he could from his early instructors and his early experience. Lewis spent all his adult life as a learner and an instructor, and much of the time he was addressing the same basic questions that John has asked in vain in book 1.

BOOK TWO

# THRILL

## Southern Adventure

Book 2 of *Pilgrim's Regress*, "Thrill," continues Lewis's dream. It traces John's journey westward, then southward, and ends with him speeding to a northern city. Book 2 has two kinds of thrill in it. First is the thrill of delivery from fear of the Landlord; second is the thrill of beautiful literature.

Characters in book 2 include the woman in the inn, Mr. Enlightenment, Vertue, Media Halfways, Mr. Halfways, and Gus Halfways. Key places include the inn, the Main Road, Claptrap, the hill, the soft lane, the old city, and the North country.

# 1

DIXIT INSIPIENS

*Atheism from Mr. Enlightenment*

This book begins with a night journey. Then comes sunrise and an inn and a woman with a broom (reminiscent of Luke 15:8–10, in which the woman stands for God seeking a lost soul), an open door, a newly lit fire, the sweeping out of old rubbish, rest, and breaking a fast. All of these images reflect things that are going to happen to John. In fact, the first five sentences of this chapter prefigure the rest of *Pilgrim's Regress* in microcosm, and a female figure named Mother Kirk (the Christian church) will eventually nurture John.

Mr. Enlightenment paraphrases a famous quotation commonly attributed to American journalist Horace Greeley (1811–1872), when he asks, "[G]oing West . . . , young man?" and takes John in tow. The title of this chapter, "Dixit Insipiens," means "The fool hath said. . . ." from the Vulgate, Psalm 53:1. The entire quotation is, of course, "The fool hath said in his heart 'There is no God.' " Mr. Enlightenment's news for John is "There is no such person."

The jolly charlatan bases his atheism on three assumptions: the clever duplicity of the Stewards, the foolish ignorance of the Stewards, and the supposed findings of modern science. His argument resembles the argument against religion Lewis had used in his teens when he presented "the recognised scientific account of the growth of religions" in a rather arrogant letter to Arthur Greeves.[1] Mr. Enlightenment is a leading

---

1. Lewis to Greeves, 12 October 1916, *They Stand Together: The Letters of C. S. Lewis to Arthur Greeves (1914–1963)*, ed. Walter Hooper (New York: Macmillan, 1979), 135.

citizen of Claptrap, the center of scientific popularizers. (Serving as a "scientific popularizer" nearly destroyed the soul of journalist Mark Studdock in *That Hideous Strength,* which Lewis published in 1945.)

"Claptrap" is a real word that means self-important, insincere, and pretentious language. It is frequently applied to shoddy work, talk, or ideas used only to win applause. A trap is a light two-wheeled carriage. It is surely not accidental that Mr. Enlightenment's cart is called a trap and his city is Claptrap. He was trying to trap John into an inadequate view of reality.

Lewis never tired of attacking Mr. Enlightenment. In 1940 he published his memorable essay "Christianity and Culture" in *Christian Reflections.* There he claimed that popularized science (not real science) encloses the poorly educated person "in a tiny windowless universe which he mistakes for the only possible universe," in which everything has been settled.[2] Lewis believed that a cultured person is almost compelled to be aware that reality is odd and that there are distant horizons and mysteries denied by popularized science. In "The Funeral of a Great Myth" (date unknown), Lewis attacks evolutionism (not evolution). Two other essays by Lewis which debunk pseudoscience are "Dogma and the Universe" (1943) and "Religion and Science" (1945).[3]

---

2. C. S. Lewis, "Christianity and Culture," *in Christian Reflections,* ed. Walter Hooper (Grand Rapids, Mich.: William B. Eerdmans Publishing, 1967), 23.
3. C. S. Lewis, *God in the Dock: Essays on Theology and Ethics,* ed. Walter Hooper (Grand Rapids, Mich.: William B. Eerdmans Publishing, 1970), 38–47, 72–75.

## 2

### THE HILL

*Vertue in Place of Religious Law*

John's joy after his "enlightenment" reflects the sentiment that Lewis expressed in a letter to Arthur Greeves in 1916. He said that he was quite content to live without believing in a bogey who was prepared to torture him forever for his failure in attaining an almost impossible ideal. Lewis assured Greeves that this is a part of Christian mythology, no matter how much Greeves tried to explain it away. "I was disappointed in my hope that you were gradually escaping from beliefs which, in my case, always considerably lessened my happiness."[4]

John bounded to the top of a bright, sunny hill—the opposite of his low, dark bedroom dominated by broken rules, and the even lower and darker black hole itself. Readers of Dante's *Inferno* are apt to see this sunrise-drenched hill as a reference to the Mount of Joy that Dante found at the beginning of his long pilgrimage away from some dark woods toward self-knowledge and God.[5] During John's peak experience of relief from fear, he perceived beauty in the eastern mountains for the first time. Similarly, some unbelievers perceive beauty in Christian tradition once they relegate it to myth and feel safe from its demands and warnings.

After his experience on the hill, John promptly came to the silly conclusion that if the world lies between a beautiful island and beautiful mountains, then all roads lead to beauty. A glance at Lewis's "Mappa Mundi" (on the endpapers of

---

4. Lewis to Greeves, 18 October 1916, *They Stand Together*, 138.
5. Dante Alighieri, *The Inferno*, canto 1, lines 13–18.

most editions) shows the irony of that idea, but of course John had no map of his world to go by.

Mr. Vertue, embodying natural human conscience, arrived as soon as John lost religious law. In Middle English, *virtue* was spelled *vertu*. The name of the hill, Jehovah-Jirah, means "God will provide." It refers to Genesis 22:14, where God provided a ram for Abraham to sacrifice in place of his son Isaac. God did not leave John to fend for himself without restraint. John still had both the robin and the sling. He was now free to shoot the robin, but he hadn't the heart for it. Desire is ruled by choice, even when religious law is missing.[6]

# 3

## A LITTLE SOUTHWARD

### *John Taken by Media Halfways*

"To travel hopefully is better than to arrive," Vertue's slogan, was a Robert Louis Stevenson quotation that Lewis scorned.[7] Lewis put it into the mouth of the Apostate Bishop in his later book *The Great Divorce* in 1945.[8] Believing in the slogan, Vertue stumped along the road with no vision of a destination, only a self-imposed sense of arbitrary duty. John, in contrast, headed South with a pretty girl in search of his Island in the realm of the arts. Media's name, of course, refers to the

---

6. For Lewis's beliefs about natural law and ethical systems such as Kant's doctrine of the categorical imperative, read his essay "On Ethics" in the collection *Christian Reflections*.
7. Robert Louis Stevenson, "El Dorado," in *Virginibus Puerisque and Other Essays* (New York: Charles Scribner's Sons, 1927), 170. See also C. S. Lewis, *Surprised by Joy: The Shape of My Early Life* (San Diego: Harcourt Brace Jovanovich, Harvest, 1966), 210–211 for Lewis's autobiographical account.
8. C. S. Lewis, *The Great Divorce* (New York: Macmillan, 1946), chap. 5, p. 37.

materials of artistic creation. Her family name indicates the insufficiency of the arts to finally satisfy.

# 4

## SOFT GOING

### *Arrival at the City of Thrill*

John believed he had found something better than his Island in the delightful romance of his journey with Media and the beauty of his meeting with her father. Mr. Halfways was priestlike and genuine. "This is the way to the *real* Island," Media promised. According to scholar Doris T. Myers, "Thrill" may be Lewis's sly reference to Clive Bell's 1927 book, *Art,* in which he claims that works of art yield "a specific thrill" which is unlike all other experiences.[9]

In his youth Lewis had believed that intense love of beauty (aesthetic sensitivity) was the best route to ultimate truth. In a 1918 letter to Arthur Greeves, Lewis stated his conviction that aesthetic "thrills" lead us to the reality of the Spirit.[10] But his 1940 essay "Christianity and Culture" explains how that idea was mistaken: "When I ask what culture has done to me personally, the most obviously true answer is that it has given me quite an enormous amount of pleasure."[11]

---

9. Doris T. Myers, *C. S. Lewis in Context* (Kent, Ohio: Kent State University Press, 1994), 15.
10. Lewis to Greeves, 29 May 1918, *They Stand Together,* 217.
11. Lewis, "Christianity and Culture," 21.

## 5

### LEAH FOR RACHEL

*Enchanted by Mr. Halfways' Song*

Again we have a chapter called "Leah for Rachel." This time John did not settle for a lusty brown girl in a forest, but for the beauty of Romantic poetry. (Mr. Halfways was much like Irish poet William Butler Yeats, whom Lewis had admired and visited.) Mr. Halfways talked about the immanence of God (the Landlord's castle is within you) but did not admit to the reality of the transcendence of God. Instead he mused, "What is truth?" which is just what Pilate asked in John 18:38 before he assented to Christ's crucifixion. When Mr. Halfways claimed, "What the imagination seizes as beauty must be truth," he was quoting a statement Romantic poet John Keats made in a letter in 1817.[12]

Mr. Halfways claimed that John already inhabited the Island, that "children of that country are never far from their fatherland," and that it is as short to the Island one way as another. (A look at the map designed by Lewis shows his opinion of this view.) Mr. Halfways' song produced a rich vision of the Island at first, but as Lewis was later to warn people, in human life "encore" is a useless word. John soon found himself more interested in his love for Media than in the Island. This is like Lewis's own search for Joy in Nordic mythology, where he was sidetracked into literary expertise. He came to call this pattern of sidetracking and correction the "dialectic of desire."[13]

---

12. John Keats, 22 November 1817, *The Selected Letters of John Keats* (New York: Farrar, Straus & Young, 1951), 88.
13. Lewis, *Surprised by Joy,* chap. 14, p. 219. See also Lewis, "Afterword to Third

## 6

### ICHABOD

*Tryst with Media Shattered*

Again Lewis has titled a disillusionment chapter "Ichabod" (the glory has departed). In book 1, chapter 5, John realized that brown girls were not what he wanted after all. This time he realized that Media was not what he wanted. Right after he had quoted John Donne's line about physical love from "The Extasie," claiming that there was something utterly unique and sublime about the love he and Media were sharing, her crude brother Gus burst in and shattered the spell.[14] He wore hobnail boots, and his mouth was shaped like the slot in a mailbox. He announced that Media was up to her usual tricks, seducing another man. Acting just like the Romantic stereotype she was, Media rushed out to commit suicide—although she would be well recovered by morning.

## 7

### NON EST HIC

*The Halfways Are Exposed*

Again Lewis has titled a chapter "Non Est Hic," referring to Luke 14:5–6, "He is not here." As before, this follows a chapter titled "The Glory Has Departed." Gus assured John that

---

Edition," in *The Pilgrim's Regress*, deluxe illustrated edition (Grand Rapids, Mich.: William B. Eerdmans Publishing, 1981), 205 (p. 10 in Lewis's 1943 preface, presented as an afterword in this edition).

14. John Donne, "The Extasie," *The Complete Poems of John Donne* (New York: Hendricks House, 1942), 34.

the Halfways were only more of the brown-girl infestation. Media looked fair, but she was brown. Gus offered to take John to Eschropolis (which means city of foul obscenity). There fantasy was out of style and real poetry, in contrast to Romantic poetry, was found in a laboratory. (John would discover later that the poetry laboratory was much like a lavatory.) John's search for the Island first detoured to a search for the real Island (poetry), and now it had detoured to a search for *real* poetry.

# 8

GREAT PROMISES

*Gus Takes John Away*

Gus, whose slang was American, considered his automobile to be poetry. He compared it to Atlanta, a mythical girl of Arcadia who would marry only the man who could outrun her, and to Apollo, the most beautiful Greek god—all in the car's favor. Gus revered technology and expense.

In 1922 American novelist Sinclair Lewis published *Babbitt,* and in 1930 he won the Nobel Prize for literature. By 1932 C. S. Lewis, who had eclectic reading habits, might have sampled the 1922 satire and noticed the beginning of chapter 3: "To George F. Babbitt, as to most prosperous citizens of Zenith, his motor car was poetry and tragedy, love and heroism."[15] *Pilgrim's Regress* is loaded with playful literary references to earlier works, and Gus was apparently C. S. Lewis's nod to George Babbitt.

In 1908 Kenneth Grahame published *The Wind in the Wil-*

---

15. Sinclair Lewis, *Babbitt* (New York: Grossett & Dunlap, 1922), 24.

*lows.* In that beloved classic, Toad was overwhelmed with passion for a motorcar. "Glorious, stirring sight!" he muttered. "The poetry of motion! . . . O bliss!" C. S. Lewis first read about Toad's poetic motorcar in *The Wind in the Willows* when he was in his late twenties.[16]

In Lewis's first draft he didn't mention John's crossing the Main Road, and he wondered if he needed to do so for clarity. Owen Barfield read the first draft and brought up that very point. In a written reply Lewis thanked him. It said much for Barfield's sagacity, Lewis told him, that he had guessed it quite right. Lewis drew a map in the letter tracing John's journey with a dotted line.[17] (As with all unpublished materials by Lewis, publication rights belong to anonymous investors who own the C. S. Lewis estate.)

John soon found himself in Gus's car racing North of the Main Road into a flat, rocky land the opposite of the "Soft Going" (Lewis's title for chapter 4) South of the Main Road. In *The Literary Legacy of C. S. Lewis,* Chad Walsh suggested that in today's terms the North might symbolize linguistic philosophy and cybernetics, and the South might symbolize drug-induced mysticism or witchcraft.[18] In his preface to *Pilgrim's Regress,* Lewis calls this motif "the dominant image of my allegory"—the barren, aching rocks of the North, the foul swamps of the South, and between them "the Road on which alone mankind can safely walk."[19]

---

16. Kenneth Grahame, *The Wind in the Willows* (New York: Charles Scribner's Sons, 1965), 38.
17. Lewis to Barfield, 2 November 1932. This letter is on display in the Wade Center at Wheaton College.
18. Chad Walsh, *The Literary Legacy of C. S. Lewis* (New York: Harcourt Brace Jovanovich, 1979), 63.
19. Lewis, "Afterword," 206 (p. 11 in preface to 1943 edition).

BOOK THREE

# THROUGH DARKEST ZEITGEISTHEIM

*Northern Misadventure*

Like the first two books of *Pilgrim's Regress,* the third one, "Through Darkest Zeitgeistheim," begins with Lewis dreaming. Here the dream becomes a nightmare. John experiences three types of "Art" in Eschropolis and learns who owns it all. Then he is imprisoned in a dungeon until the arrival of Reason with her three magic riddles. The style of book 3 moves from harsh satire and bitter comedy to fairy-tale grandeur.

Zeitgeistheim is German for home of the Spirit of the Age. (Similarly, Anaheim means home of Ana.) Lewis almost surely had in mind the popular books *Through the Dark Continent* and *In Darkest Africa* by Henry Morton Stanley. What Lewis perceived as the Spirit of the Age was a Freudian kind of reductionism that is still prevalent today.

Book 3 characters include Gus, the Clevers, Victoriana,

Phally, Glugly, Mammon, Sigismund Enlightenment, Spirit of the Age, prisoners, Master Parrot, and Reason.

In 1926 Lewis confessed to Arthur Greeves that his righteous indignation about elements in the culture of his day was dangerous because it might be making him priggish. At the time he saw no way to avoid such indignation, and in 1932 he expressed this indignation vividly in book 3 of *Pilgrim's Regress*. In 1943 he apologized in his preface to *Pilgrim's Regress* for its sometimes uncharitable tone.

# 1

## ESCHROPOLIS

### *Victoriana's Art*

Because Eschropolis was a city of filth and excrement, it was fitting that the poetry laboratory was rather like a huge bathroom. Gus introduced John by saying that he needed some cathartic music "to clean him out" because he had partaken of Romantic poetry. The Clevers gave him Victoriana's song, which spoofed Mr. Halfways, distorted John's father and the Steward as well, and conjured up a columbine flower. In the language of flowers, the columbine symbolizes folly. At the end of the song John's entire "Island" turned into one common potted houseplant.

Victoriana's song represented the experimental work of Edith Sitwell, who wrote avant-garde poems but often dressed in medieval-style gowns. Some of her early poems were near nonsense, and in 1922 her public reading of her long poem *Façade* created a sensation. The University of Texas at Austin owns a 1945 letter from Lewis to Herbert Edward Palmer stating that Victoriana was his satire of Edith Sitwell.[1]

John's lack of appreciation for Victoriana's song is similar to Lewis's poem "Spartan Nactus," published in the December 1, 1954, issue of *Punch*. It appears in *Poems* in a revised version titled "A Confession." Lewis exclaimed in mock humility that he was too insensitive to see things as contemporary poets see them. He claimed that for twenty years he had tried in vain to see an evening as "a patient etherized upon a table."[2] (T. S. Eliot described an evening that way in his famous poem "The Love Song of J. Alfred Prufrock.")[3] Lewis concluded, "I simply wasn't able."[4] He ironically classified himself as one of the dunces doomed to see life in the rich imagery and beauty of traditional views.

Because John did not praise her song, Victoriana attacked him and declared herself a victim (per-persecuted means extremely persecuted)—which supposedly proved her a great artist. As soon as "Vikky dear" left, her hypocritical friends attacked her. Their verdict *vieux jeu* meant old hat.

The Clevers sounded remarkably like the addlebrained Dufflepuds of Coriakin's Island in *The Voyage of the "Dawn Treader"* twenty years later, although they were far less likable. Lewis especially disliked the blurring of sex and age typical of the Clevers.

---

1. Joe R. Christopher, *C. S. Lewis* (Boston: G. K. Hall & Co., Twayne, 1987), 11.
2. C. S. Lewis, "A Confession," *Poems,* ed. Walter Hooper (New York: Harcourt Brace Jovanovich, Harvest, 1977), 1.
3. T. S. Eliot, *T. S. Eliot: Selected Poems* (New York: Harcourt Brace Jovanovich, 1964), 11.
4. Lewis, "A Confession," 1.

# 2

## A SOUTH WIND

### Phally's Art

The second performer, clad only in a shirt and a reptilian jock strap, performed a grossly erotic song which the Clevers greeted calmly with more trite praise. The singer demanded, "You like it, *hein?*" (In French *hein* is not a real word, but rather a *Shallbildung,* a sound that indicates something like "isn't that so" or "huh," and slightly echoes the title Zeitgeistheim.) John didn't see how rushing to black girls was any improvement upon being deceived by brown girls, since no dark girls were any satisfaction for his kind of desire.

Phally is obviously a nickname for Phallus, and Phally seems to represent D. H. Lawrence in particular. In his preface, Lewis mentioned that Lawrence had "perhaps reached a point further 'South' than humanity ever reached before."[5] In Eschropolis anyone who saw Phally's art as glorified pornography was judged primitive, puritanical, prurient, *and* repressive. Although Phally postured as a kind of wild man, all that John suffered from him was spittle in his face.

Clearly Lewis's symbolic use of brown girls and black girls is an embarrassment to many readers today. His use of dark Calormen villains twenty years later in Narnian stories also bothers some critics. It is a fact that when Lewis was less than two years old, and still called Babsie, he used to climb up on the music stool to play the piano and sing about nigger boys, to his mother's great amusement. But the adult Lewis was sen-

---

5. C. S. Lewis, "Afterword to Third Edition," in *The Pilgrim's Regress,* deluxe illustrated edition (Grand Rapids, Mich.: William B. Eerdmans Publishing, 1981), 207 (p. 12 in preface to 1943 edition).

sitive to the evil of racial prejudice and injustice. One is bound to assume that if Lewis were writing *Pilgrim's Regress* today he would choose different symbols for lust, apt as the dark-girl symbols were for a heterosexual Englishman of his day.

# 3

## FREEDOM OF THOUGHT

### *Glugly's Art*

The third performer, the essence of the ugly, could only grunt gibberish. Needless to say, Lewis was not belittling mental defectives but was attacking ugly and meaningless art. Dadaist art was a current trend that he might have had in mind; in 1944 he attacked Dadaism, along with surrealism and satanic masses.[6] Lewis would no doubt have been delighted by a professor at the University of Redlands in California who once won a poetry contest with a very obscure poem. When he received his award he explained that he had simply listed the first words of all the articles in the current issue of *Reader's Digest*, to show that much "modern" poetry is mere gibberish.

Lewis was by no means dismissing all of the unpleasant art of the 1920s as meaningless. He said in *The Personal Heresy* that the "Dirty Twenties" of our own century produced poems which succeeded in communicating moods of boredom and nausea that are real, but such moods have very small place in the life of a mature person. He did not deny that these communications were real poems, but he denied that these poets were spiritual leaders. If the poems truly reflected

---

6. C. S. Lewis, "What France Means to You," *Canadian C. S. Lewis Journal* 87 (spring 1995): 6–10.

the natures of the poets, then these poets differed from ordinary people, if at all, by defect. "They are not great souls."[7]

In contrast, the Clevers praised Glugly's nonsense as brutal satire. They claimed to be noble victims of savage disillusionment due to their suffering mud, flood, and blood. When John spoke common sense to them, they flung retorts at him and then flung worse. They beat him and chased him out of town, covering him with excrement and denouncing him as middle-class, dirty minded, and moralistic.

Clyde S. Kilby pointed out that the hard-boiled and soulless Clevers seemed to illustrate a point Lewis made in 1939 in *The Problem of Pain:* "[T]he 'frankness' of people sunk below shame is a very cheap frankness."[8]

Forty-three years after Lewis wrote about the Clevers, the thoughtful American journalist Melvin Maddocks published "Assault by Words" in the *Christian Science Monitor.* He observed that one of the favorite platitudes since 1925 was that people must be released from overcivilized restraints in order to become healthy. As Maddocks described the situation, casual obscenity has been praised as "rich, liberating, existential language." But in fact, he pointed out, glib euphemisms have been replaced by glib obscenities, and obscenity is itself a conformity. More serious than the issue of conformity, however, is the fact that obscenities, like epithets of racial prejudice, are sadistic and isolate anatomy from human wholeness. Furthermore, most obscenity degrades females. Maddocks concluded in all seriousness, "If the Watergate tapes didn't give obscenity a bad name, what

---

7. C. S. Lewis and E. M. W. Tillyard, *The Personal Heresy: A Controversy* (London: Oxford University Press, 1939), 106.
8. Clyde S. Kilby, *The Christian World of C. S. Lewis* (Grand Rapids, Mich.: William B. Eerdmans Publishing, 1964), 31, quoting Lewis, *The Problem of Pain* (London: Centenary Press, 1940), chap. 4, p. 45.

will?"[9] Readers of *Pilgrim's Regress* may have been wondering since 1933, "If the Clevers don't give obscenity a bad name, who will?"

## 4

### THE MAN BEHIND THE GUN

### *Mammon as Landlord*

In pain and exhaustion, John realized that he greatly preferred Mr. Halfways to Eschropolis. But he wanted to press on to his goal, the Island in the West. He came to Mr. Mammon (wealth), who refused to help John in any way because that would make John a welfare case. He cost John much extra walking. Mr. Mammon educated John to the fact that the Clevers were all working for him in Eschropolis, which entirely belonged to him. (Both Matthew 6:24 and Luke 16:13 quote Jesus as saying, "You cannot serve God and mammon.") So it came out that Gus Halfways, who had belittled his father for being employed by the brown girls, was himself employed by Mammon. Father for lust, and son for greed.

## 5

### UNDER ARREST

### *Caught by the Spirit of the Age*

This chapter begins with Lewis turning round in his sleep and ends with John turning round in his journey. Too tired to go on and too cold to stop, John traveled the length of a dark

9. Melvin Maddocks, "Assault by Words," *Christian Science Monitor*, 23 June 1975, 30.

valley and was blocked at the western end by guards. They would not let him go on to find the sea in order to sail to the Island in the West. This country belonged to the Spirit of the Age, and John was led back down the valley in chains.

# 6

## POISONING THE WELLS

### *The Freudian View of Reality*

John's captor was Sigismund, the son of Mr. Enlightenment. The name Sigismund refers to Sigmund Freud, of course. But it also refers to the last emperor of the Luxemburg dynasty, Sigismund (1368–1437), who treacherously promised safe conduct to John Huss, Czech forerunner of the Protestant Reformation. Sigismund had Huss imprisoned and burned at the stake in Prague in 1415. The captivity of a traveler named John by a man named Sigismund is meant to sound ominous.

Sigismund taught John that the Island was never more than a pretext for lust and that the eastern mountains are no more than wishful thinking. What John had taken for a mere pile of rocks was in fact a live stone giant—the Spirit of the Age. John began to see reality in a new way. The fact that his glimpses of the Island and the mountains had occurred at night or in a blaze of sunrise—in times of great sorrow or joy—and the fact that they were desirable were evidence that the Island and mountains did not exist.

What really existed was the massive giant. John was cast into a hillside dungeon. At this point Lewis calls his dream a nightmare for the first time. The *living stone* giant would have come to Lewis's mind because Henry Morton Stanley's famous travel books were *Through the Dark Continent, In Darkest Africa,* and *I Found Livingstone.* Even at his most serious, Lewis could be full of puns and wordplay.

It would be a waste of time to correlate each event in *Pilgrim's Regress* with Lewis's life story, except as an academic exercise. However, Lewis's reflections on Freudian reductionism in chapter 13 of *Surprised by Joy* relate closely to chapter 6. Lewis says that when he was in his early twenties the new psychology was sweeping through society and influencing everyone, although few people swallowed it whole. It made people concerned about their fantasies and wishful thinking. Lewis had lived for years with delectable mountains and western gardens as his symbols of whatever was most desirable. He always knew he didn't desire the mountains and gardens themselves. But for a time he was hoodwinked by psychoanalytic theory into thinking that he had been hoodwinked by his symbols.

# 7

FACING THE FACTS

## The Hell of Reductionism

Under the penetrating gaze of the Spirit of the Age (reductionism), John was forced to "see through" everything, including himself. All the prisoners were reduced to collections of parts—glandular and/or psychological. They became mere bundles of complexes. Because there seemed to be no escape from that hopeless view of humanity, John despaired. This cave dungeon and its concept of reality were an adaptation of

Plato's cave imagery.[10]

In 1953 Lewis returned to this theme in his Narnian story *The Silver Chair*. There Jill, Scrubb, Puddleglum, and a lost prince of Narnia were captives in the Witch's underground kingdom, where she enchanted them with a kind of reductionism. "The lamp is the real thing; the *sun* is but a tale, a children's story. . . . And look how you can put nothing into your make-believe without copying it from the real world, this world of mine, which is the only world. . . . There is no Narnia, no Overworld, no sky, no sun, no Aslan."[11]

Just in time, Puddleglum's head cleared for a moment. "Suppose we *have* only dreamed, or made up, all those things—trees and grass and sun and moon and stars and Aslan himself. Suppose we have. Then all I can say is that, in that case, the made-up things seem a good deal more important than the real ones. Suppose this black pit of a kingdom of yours *is* the only world. Well, it strikes me as a pretty poor one."[12] Then Puddleglum vowed to live and die for Aslan, and the escape of the captives began.

# 8

## PARROT DISEASE

### *Resisting Nonsense*

At last "something seemed to snap" in John's head when the jailor brought in a small pot of milk and likened it to other secretions of a cow. John spoke out against such silly reduc-

---

10. Later in *Pilgrim's Regress*, Lewis makes a direct reference to Plato's "Allegory of the Cave," quoting from it on the first page of book 10.
11. C. S. Lewis, *The Silver Chair* (New York: Macmillan, 1953), chap. 12, pp. 152, 154.
12. Ibid., 155.

tionism and was struck and dragged away as a result. Before leaving, the jailor had a model prisoner recite his lessons with his toes turned out like Tweedledum and Tweedledee in Lewis Carroll's *Through the Looking Glass*. The gist of the prisoner's lessons was that any statement can be refuted by ignoring the merits of the statement itself and accusing the speaker of saying it because of his or her (supposed) identity. If you explain *why* a person is wrong in this way, you never have to show *that* a person is wrong. In 1944 Lewis christened this kind of unreasoning argument "Bulverism." He said that for fifteen years he found the vice so common that he finally invented a name for it.[13]

It was no accident that John's jailor called reason "treason." In 1947 Lewis published a poem called "The Romantics" in the January 16 issue of the *New English Weekly*. (A revised version appears in *Poems*.)[14] The poem ends by saying that if we recall the freedom with which we used to live, the jailor calls it dope, wishful thinking, or romance. This tireless propaganda tames most people; only a few have enough strength and faith to withstand the teaching of the spirit of the age. Stone walls cannot make a prison half so secure, Lewis concluded, as a mental prison made of rigmarole.

# 9

### THE GIANT SLAYER

*Reason to the Rescue*

John was saved at the last minute by a gigantic female war-

---

13. C. S. Lewis, "Bulverism," in *God in the Dock: Essays on Theology and Ethics*, ed. Walter Hooper (Grand Rapids, Mich.: William B. Eerdmans Publishing, 1970), 271–77.
14. Lewis, "The Prudent Jailer," *Poems*, 77–78.

rior clad in steel and cloaked in blue. She entered as a captive, and then revealed her might. The Spirit of the Age knew at the sight of her that he could not withstand her, and he had to submit to her riddles. After Reason baffled and then killed the Spirit of the Age, he turned back into a pile of stone.[15]

---

15. For a study of Lewis's extraordinary poem about the virgin Reason, see appendix 2.

BOOK FOUR

# BACK TO THE ROAD

*Progress with Reason*

Book 4, "Back to the Road," begins with the guards fleeing from Reason and ends with John himself fleeing from Reason. It is the shortest but not at all the easiest book in *Pilgrim's Regress*.

## 1

### LET GRILL BE GRILL

*John's Release*

"Let Grill be Grill" refers to a character in Lewis's favorite allegory, Spenser's *Faerie Queene*. Gryll had been turned into a hog, and when a knight released him from the spell, Gryll abused the knight instead of thanking him.

"You can all come out" is the good news of book 4. This is reminiscent of John 11:43 when Jesus calls, "Lazarus, come forth." But just like a group of cynical dwarfs in *The Last*

*Battle* (1956), who stayed prisoners in the pitch-black hole of their own minds, the cynical prisoners of the Spirit of the Age chose to stay in their filthy prison.[1] Reason called their mental condition "psittacosis," which is a real parrot disease that men can catch. The prisoners parroted the falsehoods their jailor taught them. It is not accidental that Lewis chose the word psittacosis, that sounds much like neurosis and psychosis, since the prison was a kind of Freudianism.

John had enough sense to go with Reason, but she could tell that he did not have the endurance to continue all the way with her. He had a bit of Gryll in him also.

# 2

## ARCHTYPE AND ECTYPE

### *Riddle Three, about Originals and Copies*

The title "Archtype and Ectype" means the original and the copy, as discussed in Locke's *Essay Concerning Human Understanding* (1690). There Locke taught that we learn everything from our sense experience and reflection.

John's first experience after his nightmare imprisonment in the valley was a stab of Joy and a flash of the Island, all triggered by the sight of a crocus in the grass. In the language of flowers, the symbolic meaning of a crocus is youthful gladness. John's youthful gladness was restored, and at last he wept again.

Reason's dialogue with John about what she could bring from the dark part of his mind to the light part of his mind is a mysterious bit of epistemology. It may refer to material

1. C. S. Lewis, *The Last Battle* (New York: Macmillan, 1956), chap. 13, pp. 145–50.

brought up from his unconscious to his conscious mind. Of course that is merely another way of saying the same thing, although it is more common terminology (so common, in fact, that most people forget that they don't know what it really means). Lewis was deeply interested in the significance of the working of the human mind through the limitations of a physical brain.

Reason's third riddle for the Spirit of the Age had been "By what rule do you tell a copy from an original?" Reason had no simple answer to the question, but she showed John that there was no cause to assume that when two things were similar, the fair was a copy of the foul. In fact, some people thought that all our loves, be they for brown girls, for primroses, for Reason, for the Island, were copies of our love for the Landlord. In 1960 Lewis published *The Four Loves*, which discussed that very topic.

John thought that surely science has disproved such a possibility, but Reason showed him the foolishness of the ideas he had been taught by Mr. Enlightenment (whose creed was naturalism) on the first morning of his journey. Science is not equipped to teach us metaphysics. Reason's sisters Philosophy and Theology can help us to distinguish originals from copies. Reason declined to tell John the name of her father, but since he is someone John does not wish to know, we suspect that he is the Landlord.

In our generation, some scientists continue to presume to teach metaphysics. In a letter published in *Christianity Today*, Phillip E. Johnson, a professor at the University of California at Berkeley and author of *Darwin on Trial*, complained that naturalism is the true creed of today's scientific establishment, which is dominated by dedicated metaphysical naturalists. By narrowly defining reality, naturalistic scientists can pretend to explain everything.

> Contemporary science insists upon describing all of reality in naturalistic terms, which is why physicists write books with titles like *The Mind of God* and *Theories of Everything*. When Carl Sagan and Richard Dawkins preach atheism to school children in the name of science, they are rewarded for their contributions to public education by the top scientific organizations of their respective countries: Sagan with the Public Service medal of the National Academy of Sciences, and Dawkins with the Michael Faraday Award from the British Royal Society.[2]

Ironically, the great scientific genius Michael Faraday (1791–1867), pride of the Royal Society, was an intensely committed Christian.

# 3

## ESSE IS PERCIPI

### *Riddle One, about the Perception of Reality*

"Esse Is Percipi" means "To be is to be perceived," from Berkeley's *Principles of Human Knowledge* (1710). Berkeley is known for going beyond Locke, who provided the title for the previous chapter. Berkeley decided that there is no existence of matter independent of perception. He believed that the observing mind of God keeps matter in existence, and that following this line of reasoning all the way proves the existence of God.

John saw now that fair things are not always copies of foul

---

2. Phillip E. Johnson, letter to the editor, *Christianity Today*, 6 February 1995, 10, 12.

things, but he still believed that in the human mind "fair copies foul." So revulsion to self still seemed appropriate.

Reason made two points in reply. First, John must be willing to remain in doubt when he lacked sufficient evidence to decide such a question. Reason's second point resided in her first riddle to the giant, "What is the color of things in the dark?" The correct answer was no color. The Spirit of the Age could not answer that, because his trick was to pretend to expose to view things that cannot really be exposed in living people. He made people look as if they were really observable bundles of organs and bundles of complexes. In contrast, our natural level of experience is our most accurate guide to what is real. Theoretical knowledge of physiology and the unconscious is useful to physicians, and there is enough truth in that knowledge to cause a healthy humility. But that knowledge is not the most true perception of reality.

Reason's remark that John's race cannot afford to be proud is like Aslan's observation in *Prince Caspian* (1951) that to come from the line of Adam and Eve "is both honour enough to erect the head of the poorest beggar, and shame enough to bow the shoulders of the greatest emperor in earth."[3]

# 4

## ESCAPE

*Riddle Two, about Reasoning and Wishful Thinking*

The title of chapter 4, "Escape," stands for John's final escape from the chains of the Spirit of the Age, in laughter—and then his escape from Reason herself, in some haste and fear.

---

3. C. S. Lewis, *Prince Caspian* (New York: Macmillan, 1951), chap. 15, p. 180.

Riddle Two can be summed up in the old saying "Sauce for the goose is sauce for the gander." It was about a man who wanted to cross a bridge to get home, but who had his enemy at his side all the way. How could he use the bridge and keep his enemy from using it? He couldn't. This signified the fact that the Spirit of the Age wanted to use reasoning to support his own views, but unfairly denied that any other reasoning could be valid. It also signified that the Spirit of the Age called all theism mere wishful thinking, when in fact atheism can be wishful thinking also. The accusation of wishful thinking can be used either way. John's own disbelief in the Landlord was quite apt to be wishful thinking.

At this point John was on a little hill and clearly saw the old mountains of the East against the sky again. He lacked the faith he needed to follow Reason wherever she might take him, because she did not make him feel safe from the Landlord. But she had saved him from Freudian reductionism and got him headed back to the Main Road.

BOOK FIVE

# THE GRAND CANYON

## *Credibility Chasms*

Book 5, "The Grand Canyon," tells about the history of the Fall of mankind and about the inadequacy of sensible worldliness. Characters include John and Vertue, Mother Kirk, Mr. Sensible, and Drudge. There are three chasms in the story: the Grand Canyon itself, John's disbelief in Mother Kirk, and John's disillusionment with Mr. Sensible.

Mother Kirk's narrative is humble, simple, and direct. She is called by some people psychic, crazy, or witchlike. She calls herself the Landlord's daughter-in-law, but John calls her "an old creature clearly insane." Mother Kirk and Sensible utterly contradict each other. Sensible also disagrees with Reason, whom he calls "the mad woman."

Sensible's favorite themes are "the great art of life," "the secret of happiness," "comfort and amusement," "the interests of our own solid good," "joy, pleasure, ease, content," and, above all, "the good life."

# 1

## THE GRAND CANYON

### *Blocked by the Precipice of Sin*

John was reunited with Vertue where the Main Road dropped off into a deep canyon, and Vertue wanted them to dutifully risk the descent. He explained that his own rules were really the same as everyone else's, rules Lewis later called the Tao (in a special sense of that word). The basic rules of right living in all human cultures are more the same than different, Lewis said, and two of the names for this kind of decency are the natural law or the natural conscience.[1] Paul seems to refer to this natural conscience in Romans 2:12–16.

John would not try the steep descent and rejected Mother Kirk's offer to carry down the two of them (Kirk means church). But he did agree to listen to her story of the great catastrophe. It was an old wives' tale because it was no longer believed by sophisticated people and because Mother Kirk really was an old wife, in that she had been the Landlord's daughter-in-law (the bride of Christ) for almost two thousand years.

# 2

## MOTHER KIRK'S STORY

### *The Old Wives' Tale*

This is a retelling of the story of the sin of Adam and Eve. According to the "old wives' tale," the Landlord enjoyed the land with his sons and daughters. He prepared a farm for a young

---

1. C. S. Lewis, *The Abolition of Man* (New York: Macmillan, 1955), 53. See also 95–121.

couple to enjoy as permanent tenants and warned them not to eat poison wild mountain apples. The great land-grabber convinced the couple to eat a poison apple. That act caused an earthquake which swallowed their farm and left the Grand Canyon in its place. This canyon is named *Peccatum Adae,* which is from the Vulgate translation of Romans 5:12–21 and means "the sin of Adam." In the 1981 annotated Bantam edition of *Pilgrim's Regress* this reference to Adam is confused with a little-known woman named Ada invented by the poet Lord Byron, and the biblical identity of Adam is overlooked.[2]

Lewis's poem "Adam at Night," published in the May 11, 1949, issue of *Punch* and available in revised form under the title "The Adam at Night" in *Poems,* portrays how humans may have experienced their unity with the rest of the earth in a mystical way before the great catastrophe.[3]

# 3

## THE SELF-SUFFICIENCY OF VERTUE

### *Rejecting Christianity's Service and Authority*

There is no doubt that C. S. Lewis was acquainted with the Christian poetry of George Herbert (1593–1633). Surely when he recounted the old wives' tale, he had in mind Herbert's poem "Redemption."

> Having been tenant long to a rich Lord,
>    Not thriving, I resolved to be bold,

---

2. *The Pilgrim's Regress* (New York: Bantam Books, 1981), 209 n. Text notes by Dr. John C. Traupman.
3. C. S. Lewis, *Poems,* ed. Walter Hooper (New York: Harcourt Brace Jovanovich, Harvest, 1977), 45–46.

> And make a suit unto him, to afford
> A new small-rented lease, and cancell th' old.
>
> In heaven at his manour I him sought:
> > They told me there, that he was lately gone
> > About some land, which he had dearly bought
> Long since on earth, to take possession.
>
> I straight return'd, and knowing his great birth,
> > Sought him accordingly in great resorts;
> > In cities, theatres, gardens, parks, and courts:
> At length I heard a ragged noise and mirth
>
> Of theeves and murderers: there I him espied,
> > Who straight, *Your suit is granted*, said, and died.[4]

After a rude question from John about the rules and the black hole, Mother Kirk continued her story. Since the great earthquake, the wild apple was grafted onto all other trees, and so all fruit is infected with the poison. The Steward's list of rules is needed to help people keep healthy, because all their food is more or less harmful.

Vertue refused Mother Kirk's assistance in crossing the gorge on principle, quoting the conclusion of William Ernest Henley's poem "Invictus."

> Out of the night that covers me,
> > Black as the Pit from pole to pole,
> I thank whatever gods may be
> > For my unconquerable soul.

---

4. Peter Levi, ed., *The Penguin Book of English Christian Verse* (New York: Viking Penguin, Penguin Books, 1988), 100–101.

> In the fell clutch of circumstance
> > I have not winced nor cried aloud.
> Under the bludgeonings of chance
> > My head is bloody, but unbowed.
>
> Beyond this place of wrath and tears
> > Looms but the Horror of the shade,
> And yet the menace of the years
> > Finds, and shall find, me unafraid.
>
> It matters not how strait the gate,
> > How charged with punishments the scroll,
> I am the master of my fate;
> > I am the captain of my soul.[5]

In his pride, Vertue told Mother Kirk he wanted to use his own legs—an intentional irony on Lewis's part because Henley was so severely crippled that he was a semi-invalid. Because Vertue seemed to symbolize self-reliance, unyielding moral strength, and the determination to do not what one likes but what one chooses, Chad Walsh thought that today Vertue could be labeled Mr. Existential.[6]

John agreed with Vertue because he was fearful. Mother Kirk said correctly that if they made the descent alone, she might encounter them as they faced the ascent on the other side.

It is worth remembering that Lewis wrote this story in the house of Arthur Greeves in August 1932. In 1930, Lewis had started a letter to Greeves in which he dwelt a great deal upon his own conceit and self-will, spelling out the seven deadly

---

5. William Ernest Henley, "Invictus," in *The Norton Anthology of English Literature*, 5th ed., ed. M. H. Abrams (New York: W. W. Norton & Co., 1986), 2:1657.
6. Chad Walsh, *The Literary Legacy of C. S. Lewis* (New York: Harcourt Brace Jovanovich, 1979), 66.

sins in Latin and claiming *superbia* (pride), not cowardice, as his own worst flaw and "the mother of all sins." He likened himself to a musical instrument that prefers to play itself because it thinks it knows the tune better than the Musician. (Lewis pointed out in the same letter that Greeves suffered mainly from *accidia*—laziness—and that Greeves was more like a musical instrument that is unstrung.)[7] Thus Vertue's sin in this allegory was the one Lewis had confessed to in real life.

## 4

### MR. SENSIBLE

### *Appeal of "The Good Life"*

The pair made Mr. Sensible their willing host. He was rather a favorite of Lewis's. Lewis hoped that as well as allegory, he had a touch of mythical life about him. Mr. Sensible is a scatterbrain who hides his ignorance behind a cascade of seemingly erudite quotations. His conversation in chapters 3 and 4 is sprinkled with Greek, Latin, and French phrases, not always correctly rendered. By the end of chapter 4 Mr. Sensible has lapsed into gibberish (mildly foreshadowing the "Banquet at Belbury" chapter in *That Hideous Strength*). Mr. Sensible's quotations are not to be taken seriously, and Lewis told Arthur Greeves that translations aren't needed.[8] The dialogue is meant to show that Sensible's quotations were always silly and he always missed the point of the authors he quoted. But the following meanings, primarily from Henry Noel, interest some readers.

---

7. Lewis to Greeves, 30 January 1930, *They Stand Together: The Letters of C. S. Lewis to Arthur Greeves (1914–1963)*, ed. Walter Hooper (New York: Macmillan, 1979), 342.
8. Lewis to Greeves, 17 December 1932, *They Stand Together,* 447.

*Regum oequabit opes animis*—He is equal to a king in the riches of the spirit (Virgil *Georgics* 4.132).

*Omnes eodem cogimur*—We are all being gathered to the same fold (Horace *Odes* 2.3.25).

*Quo dives Tullus et Ancus*—We descend to the land of the dead, where rich Tullus and Ancus have gone (Horace *Odes* 4.7.15).

*Nullius addictus*—I do not take sides; I am not bound to swear by the statement of any authority (Horace *Epistles* 1.2.14).

*En deshabille*—a state of undress (French).

*J'aime le jeu . . .*—I like games, love, books, music, town and country—everything, in fact! (Jean de la Fontaine, *Psyche* 1.2).

*Haud equidem invideo*—I don't hold it against you by any means (Virgil *Eclogues* 1.11).

*Caelum non animum mutamus*—We change the scenery, not ourselves (Horace *Epistles* 1.11.27).

*Et ego in Arcadia!*—I too was (or am) in Arcadia. This anonymous line is found on numerous tombs, and also on paintings which include tombs (such as works by Ranolommeo Schidoni, Nicolas Poussin, and Sir Joshua Reynolds). The line is usually interpreted to mean: "I also have lived in Arcady, a lovely rural place in Greece; therefore I also am an idealist." It has also been taken to mean either "I, the dead person, though in the tomb am still in Arcady," or "I, Death, come even to Arcady."

*μονόχρονος ἡδονή*—momentary or fleeting pleasure (Greek).

*Eadem sunt omnia semper*—Everything remains ever the same (Latin).

*Le bon sens*—common sense (French).

*Auream quisquis*—the man who cherishes the golden mean (Horace *Odes* 2.10.5).

*Do manus!*—I give up/surrender (Latin).

*Que sais-je?*—What do I know? (Montaigne, motto on his personal seal).

Sensible claimed that the wine he produced himself surpassed the flavor of the sacred fountain touched by Pegasus. He quoted Virgil, "He is equal to a king in the riches of the spirit," and then mentioned that his dog Rover would be exterminated soon. To justify that, he quoted from Horace's *Odes*, "We are all being gathered to the same fold," and made reference to the land of the dead. Rover was only an expendable object to him, he explained. (Lewis had tolerated the senile eccentricities of his extremely old dog named Tim for years and years.)

Mr. Sensible paused to call his servant a foul name and then continued his "good conversation" with John and Vertue. Sensible's idea of good conversation was a monologue in which he carelessly mixed scraps of ideas from many writers.

He quoted Horace about "not taking sides" and said he liked to explore his guests' minds "in informal dress."

Almost twenty years after he wrote *Pilgrim's Regress,* Lewis wrote to his American correspondent William Kinter that Mr. Sensible is the type of person of which Montaigne was the best literary specimen. Inferior examples among writers would be Horace, Lord Chesterfield, Walter Pater, Matthew Arnold (as a critic, not as a poet), George Saintsbury, Professor Walter Raleigh, and George Gordon.[9]

When Sensible learned that the two wanted to cross the Canyon he quoted Virgil's *Eclogues,* "I don't hold it against you by any means," but he agreed with Horace in his *Epistles,* "We change the scenery, not ourselves." When he learned that John was seeking the Island in the West, he quoted an old Latin tomb inscription, "I too was in Arcady," and warned him that we must discipline our imaginations in the interests of "our own solid good." That last phrase takes on a special irony later in John's journey.

Sensible valued the art of enjoying but being unattached to fleeting pleasure, and he said so in Greek. He also liked pleasure detached from its natural context, just as he constantly quoted phrases out of context. Thus he praised the Roman practice of inducing vomiting at banquets for the sake of gluttony, and the use of contraceptives for the sake of lust.

Sensible quoted Pope's maxim "The proper study of mankind is man" as a reason for ignoring the Canyon. (In Lewis's revised poem "The Prudent Jailer" the jailer claims "the proper study of prisoners is prison.")[10] Sensible assured John

---

9. Lewis to Kinter, 30 July 1954, C. S. Lewis Letters to Miscellaneous Correspondents, index no. 727–771D, Marion E. Wade Center, Wheaton College, Wheaton, Ill.
10. First published as "The New Romantics" in *The New English Weekly* 30 (16 January 1947): 130. Revised version published as "The Prudent Jailer" in *Poems,* 77, and *The Collected Poems of C. S. Lewis,* ed. Walter Hooper (London: HarperCollins, 1994), 91.

that places are always the same. He detested Reason, preferring common sense—which seeks comfort instead of truth. He would lock Reason in jail if he could. He referred to Aristotle as his teacher and started to quote Horace about the golden mean, but Vertue interrupted to correct him.

"I give up!" Mr. Sensible exclaimed, and begged Vertue not to be pedantic; but Vertue, lacking the social graces, continued to correct Sensible about Aristotle. Sensible replied with "the old refrain," Montaigne's personal motto, "What do I know?" and insisted that philosophy should be merely decorative. He said that he had gone to the Porch (teaching place of Zeno) and the Academy (teaching place of Plato) as a spectator, not a participant. At last Lewis dreamed them all to the dining table.

# 5

## TABLE TALK

### *Hypocrisy of "The Good Life"*

The chapter title "Table Talk" is the title of Martin Luther's famous little book, but Sensible's table talk is quite different from Luther's. Again Mr. Sensible quotes some classical authors:

> *Dapibus mensas onerabat inemptis*—He loaded his table with delicacies not bought at the store (Virgil *Georgics* 4.133). This is a continuation of the *Regum* passage of the previous chapter.

> *Αθανάντους μέν* . . .—The most important thing is to honor the gods as is required by the law (Pythagoras).

*Cras ingens iterabimus*—Tomorrow we shall sail upon the boundless sea (Horace *Odes* 1.7.32). From "O you brave heroes, who with me have often suffered worse misfortunes, now banish cares with wine. Tomorrow we will sail the vast sea again."

*Pellite cras ingens tum-tum . . .*—a nearly meaningless and drunken mixture of Latin and Greek. According to Clyde Kilby in *Images of Salvation,* a hazard at translation might result in "Drive out the great tomorrow tum-tum as the law demands."

When Lewis was twenty-three he recorded in his journal that at supper he drank cowslip wine for the first time in his life. He described it as "green in colour, bittersweet, as warming as good sherry, but heavy in its results and a trifle rough on the throat—not a bad drink."[11] The cowslip is a yellow primrose, the flower John first encountered greedily as a toddler. In the language of flowers, cowslip is the symbol of pensiveness. John began his supper with Mr. Sensible by drinking some of this wildflower beverage that Sensible praised so highly, and John didn't like it.

Sensible quoted from Virgil's *Georgics,* "He loaded his table with delicacies not bought at the store." But only the primrose wine and the radishes (Sensible quoted Cowper on radishes) were his own produce. John didn't know where the rest came from, but Lewis knew all the free sources in his dream. (Hock, claret, and port were wines served after the cowslip wine, sherry, and champagne.) Lewis also knew that Epicurus, who taught that the highest good is pleasure, was

---

11. C. S. Lewis, 28 June 1922, *All My Road Before Me: The Diary of C. S. Lewis 1922–1927,* ed. Walter Hooper (San Diego: Harcourt Brace Jovanovich, 1991), 59–60.

founder of the house itself.

Mr. Sensible, rather drunk, included thanks to the Landlord in Latin as one more pleasurable element of the meal, a matter of style, then ended his increasingly inebriated monologue with an unintelligible mixture of Latin and Greek.

# 6

### DRUDGE

### *Fragility of "The Good Life"*

Unable to sleep in such a cold house, John wandered out and learned from Drudge that Sensible's unproductive garden was not only all rock, but also constantly slipping down into the gorge. The miserable Drudge himself had served there since Epicurus and was once called "Subsidy" rather than Drudge. Now he felt ready to quit his job and head North.

# 7

### THE GAUCHERIE OF VERTUE

### *The End of "The Good Life"*

Vertue's gaucherie (gaucheness) was his tactlessness in pointing out Mr. Sensible's hypocrisy and pretenses. Mr. Sensible had to admit that his gracious life depended entirely upon his health, his wealth, and the service of others. Deserted by Drudge, he meant to practice "self-sufficiency" in a hotel until he obtained modern machines to replace Drudge. If such machines were not yet available, he would obtain slaves created by geneticists—humans who work like machines.

When Sensible realized that Drudge was heading North with John and Vertue, he said, "Hurrah for nonsense!" and claimed that his house was named something like *Choice,* and its motto "Do what you will." (What Sensible willed was to get himself some slaves.)[12]

---

12. The hypocritical Mr. Sensible seems "singularly solid and four-square," as Vertue reflects in book 10. But the insubstantial nature of Mr. Sensible and his concept of "our own solid good" were foreshadowed in C. S. Lewis's ironic unfinished novel, "The Most Substantial People" (1927). (See Kathryn Lindskoog, *Light in the Shadowlands: Protecting the Real C. S. Lewis* [Sisters, Oreg.: Multnomah Books, 1994], chap. 5, 107–124.) The "most substantial people" lived in a fictitious section of Belfast named *Wanhope* Gardens. In the last paragraph of his preface to *Pilgrim's Regress,* Lewis explains that the island named *Wanhope* in his map on the endleaves is part of a half-whimsical attempt to fill in the "Northern" half of the world with appropriate spiritual phenomena: *"Wanhope* is Middle English for Despair." Mr. Sensible foreshadows the insubstantial souls who reject their own solid good in heaven in *The Great Divorce* (1945). And the insubstantial souls in *The Great Divorce* resemble the phantom souls that Dante described in *The Inferno.* Lewis's "substantial people" in 1927, his Mr. Sensible in 1932, and his tourists in 1945 are all manifestations of his lifelong drive to penetrate appearances and perceive what is real rather than transitory. Lewis expressed this drive very differently in his 1956 essay "Behind the Scenes," now available in *God in the Dock,* and in his 1963 essay "The Seeing Eye," now available in *Christian Reflections.*

BOOK SIX

# NORTHWARD ALONG THE CANYON

## To the Utter North in Vain

Book 6, "Northward along the Canyon," tells of John's visit at a bleak northern commune dedicated to counter-Romanticism. Vertue goes on to the North to find that there is no crossing of the canyon there; and he returns to warn of great danger. Characters in book 6 are John, Vertue, Drudge, Angular, Classical, Humanist, and Savage. Lewis expressed regret in his 1943 preface that the tone of book 6 is sometimes bitter.

In 1939 Lewis discussed book 6 in a letter to his friend Sister Penelope (at an Anglican convent in Wantage). He explained that the Tableland represents "*all* high and dry states of mind," including High Anglicanism.[1] In 1932 most of the High Anglicans Lewis had encountered were harsh people who called themselves scholastics and appeared to be inspired

---

1. Lewis to Sister Penelope, 8 November 1939, *Letters of C. S. Lewis,* edited and with a memoir by W. H. Lewis, revised and enlarged edition edited by Walter Hooper (San Diego: Harcourt, Brace & Co., Harvest, 1993), 327–28.

more by hatred of their fathers' religion than anything else. By 1939 Lewis had modified that view somewhat, but he was still not a High Anglican. To Lewis the real distinction was not between high and low (closer to the Roman Catholic Church or farther from it), but between religion with a real supernaturalism and salvationism on the one hand, and all watered-down and modernist versions on the other.

# 1

## FIRST STEPS TO THE NORTH

### Desolate March Northward

This time John did not have Gus Halfways' auto to speed him on a stony trip northward. He had to lean on Vertue and Drudge on the cold uphill journey.

# 2

## THREE PALE MEN

### The Community against Mystical Nonsense

In his 1943 preface Lewis apologized for this chapter, which he called a "preposterous allegorical filigree."[2] He may have got the basic idea for this "filigree" from his rather wry interest in 1930 in a communal experiment by three idealistic young men, including his ex-student Bede Griffiths. They were supported by an inheritance that one of them had

---

2. C. S. Lewis, "Afterword to Third Edition," in *The Pilgrim's Regress*, deluxe illustrated edition (Grand Rapids, Mich.: William B. Eerdmans Publishing, 1981), 208 (p. 13 in preface to 1943 edition).

received. The trio led a frugal, studious life in a Cotswold cottage and tried to avoid all products of industry.

John, Vertue, and Drudge arrived at the shed of three unpleasant brothers, sons of Mr. Enlightenment of Claptrap. Their mother was Mr. Enlightenment's second wife, Euphuia (good disposition). Vertue revealed that he was an older son of the same Euphuia, but he didn't know who his father was. His three half-brothers weren't interested. They had been reared by their other half-brother, Sigmund (Sigismund), who was born to Mr. Enlightenment's first wife, Epichaerecacia (gloating). As they were educated, these three observed that visitors to Mr. Halfways always became enslaved to Media in Thrill or else moved on to Eschropolis, and moving to Eschropolis always led to the giant's dungeon. They hated all three places: Thrill, Eschropolis, and the dungeon. That hatred bound them together.

The brothers brought forth an extremely skimpy meal. (Bully beef is simply canned beef.) Depressing as their fare was, Drudge spoke for a large part of our world when he commented, "It's better than radishes, sir."

The young cleric Neo-Angular had rebuffed Vertue, who was an honest pagan, by quoting Tertullian: *"Virtutes paganorum splendida vitia,"* which means, "The virtues of the pagans are splendid vices." But Angular dutifully shared his small geometrical meal with all three visitors. Both Angular and Vertue dutifully took as little as possible. In contrast, Classical and Humanist dutifully declined to share any of their food, since that was against their principles. Although those four were motivated by duty, John and Drudge were motivated by hunger.

Snobbish attitudes were obvious in all three brothers. Mr.

Neo-Classical, a religious agnostic, praised the form of the pieces of food (he was concerned with outer shape, not essence) and referred disparagingly to the kickshaws (tidbits) of "lower countries." Classical disbelieved in the pleasant land across the gorge. According to Chad Walsh, Classical is a caricature of Irving Babbitt, an American scholar who vigorously opposed Romanticism and died in 1933. Angular believed in the country across the gorge, but otherwise he and Classical generally agreed about important matters; they considered themselves bravely realistic. Chad Walsh points out that Angular is a caricature of T. S. Eliot. Eliot's well-known Anglo-Catholicism is suggested by Angular's name, but it is Eliot's dry anti-Romantic approach to literature as well as religion that Lewis is satirizing.

In June 1926 Lewis dreamed up a satirical literary hoax intended to trick Eliot.[3] In 1942 he explained his objection to Eliot's "penitential" style.

> If Mr. Eliot disdains the eagles and trumpets of epic poetry because the fashion of this world passes away, I honour him. But if he goes on to draw the conclusion that all poetry should have the penitential qualities of his own best work, I believe he is mistaken. As long as we live in merry middle earth it is necessary to have middle things. . . . Mr. Eliot may succeed in persuading the reading youth of England to have done with robes of purple and pavements of marble. But he will not therefore find them walking in sackcloth on floors of mud—he will only find them in smart, ugly suits walking on rubberoid. It has all been tried before. The older Puritans took away

---

3. See pages 410–414 in *All My Road Before Me: The Diary of C. S. Lewis,* ed. Walter Hooper (San Diego: Harcourt Brace Jovanovich, 1991).

the maypoles and the mince-pies: but they did not bring in the millennium, they only brought in the Restoration.[4]

And in 1954 he repeated his objection in verse, gently mocking both Eliot's poetry and his response to it.[5]

Humanist was an atheist who lived to oppose optimism, Romanticism, transcendentalism, and humanitarianism. (It was a Clever in Eschropolis who said he had "got over his humanitarianism" when he kicked John on the kneecap.) Humanist also opposed yearning and ecstasy (Nympholepsy), agreeing in part with the Spirit of the Age and Mr. Sensible. Nevertheless, Humanist seemed blindly optimistic, because he expected to develop a tolerably comfortable community in the future. According to Chad Walsh, Humanist is a thinly disguised George Santayana.[6]

3

NEO-ANGULAR

*Dry Intellectual Christianity*

Mr. Angular insisted that John spend the day at his hut—not out of hospitality or human kindness, which he disdained, but in obedience to rules. Angular actually believed that Mother Kirk could carry John across the canyon, but he insisted that John's Island had to be part of the land of destruction on his own side of the canyon. And everything

---
4. C. S. Lewis, *A Preface to "Paradise Lost"* (New York: Oxford University Press, Galaxy, 1961), 137.
5. See "Spartan Nactus" on page 685 of the December 1954 issue of *Punch*. A revised version of that poem appears under the title "A Confession" on page 1 of Lewis's *Poems,* ed. Walter Hooper (San Diego: Harcourt Brace Jovanovich, Harvest, 1977).
6. Chad Walsh, *The Literary Legacy of C. S. Lewis* (New York: Harcourt Brace Jovanovich, 1979), 68.

East of the canyon was "much of a muchness" (a British idiom for interchangeable).

When John countered Angular with Mother Kirk's and Reason's teaching, Angular insisted that John was incapable of really understanding either woman. But John realized that in casually condemning both the city of Thrill and the Island, Angular was speaking out of arrogant personal ignorance. John attacked Angular for his unwillingness to withhold judgment, the very lesson that John had recently learned from Reason. John was angry.

Lewis said in his preface that what put him out of patience was the scorn which claimed to be from above. Some people condemn what they do not even understand. When critics called Romanticism "nostalgia," Lewis felt that their mistaken idea that the desired object was in the past put them in the category of people who teach about geometry but who have not yet themselves come to the first difficult theorem in geometry, the *Pons Asinorum*.[7] This dismissal of Romanticism made Lewis lose his temper.

In the midst of John's angry outburst to Angular, there is a misprint that has mysteriously endured for over fifty years of printings. John seems to say to Angular, "I know this by experience as I know a dozen things about it *which of you* [italics added] betray your ignorance as often as you speak." But in fact Lewis wrote, "I know this by experience as I know a dozen things about it *of which you* [italics added] betray your ignorance as often as you speak."

---

7. C. S. Lewis, "Afterword," 205 (pp. 10–11 in preface to 1943 edition).

## 4

### HUMANIST

*Sterility of Worldly Humanism*

Humanist's garden was strictly geometrical and inert. As Humanist's meal was free from romantic sauces, his garden was free from signs of life. He boasted of this condition as if it were a matter of choice, scorning the shapes of potatoes and cabbages. He claimed that he was pioneering, but he conceded that his hopes of future productivity on this stone tableland were part of a graceful veil of illusion.

## 5

### FOOD FROM THE NORTH

*Vertue Returns*

At the end of the day Vertue returned from the far North with a meat pie, beer, rum for grog, and a warning of great danger.

## 6

### FURTHEST NORTH

*Warning of Imminent Northern Scourge*

Not much over fifteen miles North, Vertue and Drudge had come to a valley of dwarfs—Fascists and Communists (Marxomanni). Drudge joined the latter group, the red dwarfs, immediately. ("It's better than radishes, sir.") Vertue went on up the honeycombed mountain to meet the ruler of the land, Savage. He was a Nordic warrior much like Odin, god of war. His wife Grimhild was Media Halfways' older sister. She was a murderous character Lewis borrowed from *The Nibelungenlied*, a German epic poem probably written around A.D. 1200 at the latest. "Grim" means hooded and "hild" means warrior.

Savage sang lines from the ancient Icelandic *Elder Edda* and drank and ate and shouted as well. He told of his dwarf warriors called Mussolimini (Italian Fascists), Swastici (Hitler had just been elected chancellor of Germany when Lewis wrote this), Gangomanni (gangsters), and many others: the Cruels. With these legions Savage planned to destroy the land; he and Grimhild would drink blood from the skulls of Humanist and Classical. All who built for happiness and security, he claimed, were fools. Since this is a world of destruction, he planned to be a destroyer rather than a mere victim of destruction. Heroic violence was all that counted.

## 7

FOOLS' PARADISE

*Mental Softness of the Tough-Minded*

Angular responded cheerfully that Savage must be a clear thinker. Humanist decided happily that Savage was the epitome of all that Humanism stood against, and so Savage enhanced the importance of Humanist, whose intelligence would be adequate defense against any armed attacks. Classical simply disbelieved that Savage existed. And so to sleep all.

Just seven years after Lewis wrote this chapter, Hitler invaded Poland. Lewis and some friends got the bad news when they were on a vacation in Warren Lewis's cabin cruiser on the Thames. Robert E. Havard, Lewis's doctor as well as one of his friends, recalled that in the overshadowing gloom at dinner that evening Lewis said semiseriously, "Well, at any rate, we now have less chance of dying of cancer."[8]

In the middle of January in the dark year of 1940 Lewis wrote to his friend Bede Griffiths that Fascism and Communism, like all other evils, have power because of the good they contain or pretend to contain. The reason they make progress is that people have failed to provide for each other the good that these seemingly offer. Lewis saw both Fascism and Communism as very bad systems, and he feared that both would penetrate Christianity by way of the good they seem to offer humanity. "Mark my words," Lewis warned, "you will frequently see both a Leftist and Rightist pseudo-theology developing." Referring to the desecration of the temple in Jerusalem that Jesus warned about in Matthew 24:15, Lewis concluded his remarks about extremist politics invading the church by stating, "The abomination will stand where it ought not." His very next paragraph, however, was about our duty to try as hard as we can to obey the scriptural commandment "Rejoice always."[9] During the war, this duty had become one of Lewis's highest priorities.

One evening after the fall of France in June 1940, when the invasion of England seemed imminent, Lewis and some of his friends were thinking of passages in their writings that could

---

8. Robert E. Havard, "Philia: Jack at Ease," in *C. S. Lewis at the Breakfast Table and Other Reminiscences,* ed. James T. Como (New York: Macmillan, 1979), 220.
9. Lewis to Griffiths, 17 January 1940, *Letters of C. S. Lewis,* 336.

mark them for extermination under Nazi occupation. Lewis recalled vividly his black dwarfs in black shirts, the inhuman subspecies called Swastici. As Havard put it, that was not their happiest evening.[10]

---

10. Havard, "Philia," 220.

BOOK SEVEN

# SOUTHWARD ALONG THE CANYON

*Southward to Human Wisdom*

Book 7, "Southward along the Canyon," includes three pages of Mr. Broad saying, "Dear me... We are none of us perfect," and fifteen pages of Wisdom's metaphysics and philosophy. Thus we move from absolute nonsense to Absolute Idealism, from the bland niceties of the liberal church to the rigorous teaching of idealistic philosophy.

Characters in book 7 include John and blind, sick Vertue, Mr. Broad and Martha, and Wisdom with his many children.

## 1

### VERTUE IS SICK

*Traditional Morality Is Now Undone*

When John and Vertue departed from the "high and dry" home of the three brothers, the consistent weather in that region was "clouds and wind without rain." Lewis was evidently referring to Proverbs 25:14, "Like clouds and wind without rain is one who boasts of a gift never given." The three cold, windy, boastful brothers gave no wisdom to John and Vertue.

Vertue's experiences had undermined his complacent dedication to duty which had no apparent meaning. He wondered what rigid self-discipline was really good for. After his visit to warlike Savage, he wondered if his self-discipline was all training for some future life-or-death battle. Eventually Vertue's despairing words would prove true in a positive sense, but at this point Vertue was sickened by the nihilism of Savage.

Vertue was fanatically dedicated to remaining uninfluenced by rewards and punishments. They would, he felt, destroy his integrity. Unlike John, he had remained unmoved by fear and desire. But now he realized that he didn't know how to make any choices he liked. Now Vertue was not only unmoved by fear and desire, but also paralyzed by a sense of futility. He disappeared like a phantom, and John wondered for the first time if Vertue was real. Searching for him was a wasted effort.

# 2

## JOHN LEADING

### *Vertue Struck Dumb and Blind*

John wept for the first time since shortly after Reason had released him from the Spirit of the Age. The weeping strengthened him, and once he resumed his journey he found Vertue. Lewis says that he was quick to understand in his dream, but John was slow to understand in his experience, that Vertue was now blind and helpless. In the headline Lewis quotes Wordsworth's *Prelude:* "Sick, wearied out with contrarieties, he yields up moral questions in despair."

# 3

## THE MAIN ROAD AGAIN

### *They Face the South*

John and blind Vertue returned to the South, where they found sunshine, birdsong, earthy food, and sleep.

# 4

## GOING SOUTH

### *An Easier Path*

John and Vertue wound their way down a pleasant, literally primrose path to the charming house of Mr. Broad, the book's third Steward. Mr. Broad welcomed the pair with "Come in, come in," and gently echoed himself for the rest of their visit.

# 5

## TEA ON THE LAWN

### *Mr. Broad, the Liberal Church*

Mr. Broad had been tutored by Mr. Enlightenment in his youth and claimed Mr. Sensible as his oldest friend. Mr. Broad lived with his wife or housekeeper, Martha, reminding readers of Luke 10:38–42, in which Martha busied herself with the duties of gracious hospitality while her sister Mary more wisely sat and learned from Jesus.

Mr. Broad was nothing if not affable, and he used the word *dear* eight times in their brief exchange. He also used words like *splendidly, delightful,* and *love.* He separately excused Mr. Sensible, Mother Kirk, and Wisdom for their foibles with his generous "We are none of us perfect." He twisted the meaning of 1 Corinthians 13:11 about putting away childish things and 1 Kings 8:27 about God not being contained in a house built by man.

Broad's main point was that Mother Kirk is rather out-of-date and that the beauty of nature is a truer teacher today. He wanted to launch into talk about botany as a window on the Infinite, but John was not interested. Lewis added a helpful note in his 1943 headline about Mr. Broad being fond of wildflowers. He expected readers to realize that he was referring to William Blake's famous quatrain in "Auguries of Innocence," written circa 1800:

> To see a World in a Grain of Sand
> And a Heaven in a Wild Flower
> Hold Infinity in the palm of your hand
> And Eternity in an hour[1]

Rather than going through the trouble of a pilgrimage, Mr. Broad believed one could find heaven all around in the beauty of nature.

Lewis began his preface to *The Great Divorce* in 1945 by assuring readers that he did not think himself a fit antagonist for so great a genius as Blake, and that he was not even sure

---

1. William Blake, "Auguries of Innocence," from the Pickering Manuscript, *William Blake: The Complete Poems,* ed. Alicia Ostriker (New York: Penguin Books, 1986), stanza 1, p. 506.

he understood Blake.² But he was sure that no new development, adjustment, or refinement would somehow turn evil into good (as Mr. Broad seemed to insist). John refused to settle for wild primroses; he insisted upon his Island.

# 6

## THE HOUSE OF WISDOM

### Arriving at Idealistic Philosophy

After traveling through a more noble landscape along a river, John and Vertue arrived at a broad lawn and the house of Wisdom, where they were welcomed to wholesome and simple fare. There at last John collected himself and reviewed his history, then fell into deep sleep.

# 7

## ACROSS THE CANYON BY MOONLIGHT

### To the Island in a Dream

In 1930, Lewis wrote to Arthur Greeves that for imaginative people it is fatally easy to confuse an aesthetic appreciation of the spiritual life with the life itself. It is similar to dreaming that one has waked, washed, and dressed, only to find oneself still in bed,³ an experience that was especially vivid in Lewis's mind because he had recently read George MacDonald's *Princess and the Goblin* for the third time. In the twenty-seventh chapter, "The Goblins in the King's House," MacDonald told

2. C. S. Lewis, *The Great Divorce* (New York: Macmillan, 1946), 5.
3. Lewis to Greeves, 15 June 1930, *They Stand Together: The Letters of C. S. Lewis to Arthur Greeves (1914–1963)*, ed. Walter Hooper (New York: Macmillan, 1979), 361.

how the hero thought he had jumped up and begun to dress, but found he was still in bed.

"Now then I will!" he said. "Here goes! I *am* up now!"

But he discovered again that he was snug in bed. Twenty times he tried, and twenty times he failed, because he was only dreaming he was awake.[4]

John dreamed that he crossed the Grand Canyon and approached the Island. This was his first glimpse of the Island since Reason had delivered him from the Spirit of the Age. This time his female companion was a darkly clothed shadow of contemplation instead of the bright warrior. Here John's dream was within Lewis's fictional dream about John, of course; a dream within a dream.

# 8

## THIS SIDE BY SUNLIGHT

### *Idealism Denies the Reality of the Island*

Wisdom warned John and Vertue that they must utterly rid themselves of the superstitious southern error, belief in literal supernatural religion. On the other hand, they must avoid the more northern error of materialism, the belief that other-worldly realities are only illusions. Joe Christopher points out that Wisdom's dismissal of materialism was typical of Lewis.

> There are certain things in the world that cannot be explained as products of the world: in this allegory, the roads of the country, the Landlord's (God's) and each man's inner rules, and the Island in the West seen by

---

4. George MacDonald, *The Princess and the Goblin* (Philadelphia: J. B. Lippincott Co., 1935), 267.

John. Therefore, the universe must be ultimately mental, not physical, for parts of it cannot be explained physically. According to the headnote of the 1943 edition, the roads stand for logical categories (it does not seem the best symbolism) and the rules for moral values.[5]

There is a middle way which is true.

The idea of this middle way created in John an inner comfort expressed in the most ironic sentence in *Pilgrim's Regress:* "Some fear was removed: the suspicion, never before wholly laid at rest, that his wanderings might lead him soon or late into the power of the Landlord, had passed away."

Later that day John was taught that the house of Wisdom is partway down the canyon in the Valley of Humiliation (Bunyan's term), and that it is impossible to cross the deeper crevasse. Furthermore, there is not an actual place one could get to even if one could cross. It is wise for a person to desire the far side, but it is not wise for a person to hope for fulfillment of such a desire.

The house of Wisdom resembles Limbo, on the edge of the great pit in canto 4 of Dante's *Inferno*. There on a green meadow Dante came to the wise and virtuous pagans: "You don't ask who these are? I want you to know, before you go any farther, that they were not evildoers. Although they were virtuous, that was not enough, because they were not baptised into the Christian faith. Some, living before Christianity, did not worship God adequately, and I am one of these. For such faults and no other, we are lost; and this is our only suffering: to be cut off from all hope, yet to live on in desire."[6] At the house of Wisdom, that is what John was told: "It is not

---

5. Joe R. Christopher, *C. S. Lewis* (Boston: G. K. Hall & Co., Twayne, 1987), 12.
6. Dante Alighieri, *The Inferno*, canto 4, lines 31–42 (unpublished prose translation by Kathryn Lindskoog). At the beginning of book 7, Lewis quotes part of the same

desire that [Wisdom's] doctrine kills: it is only hope."

## 9

### WISDOM—EXOTERIC

*Idealism Endorses the "Other and Outer"*

The chapter title "Wisdom—Exoteric" means readily understood wisdom. In this chapter John learns the idealist view of reality during his second lesson from Wisdom.

Wisdom refuted the giant and affirmed Reason. He assured John that the Island is not a disguise for lust, because an adolescent boy can see through that mistake in two years. (Wisdom is referring to Lewis.) Wisdom mentioned in passing that some Stewards claim that John's Island is a blurred and confused sight of the Landlord's castle from far off. But Wisdom had already dismissed the Landlord as a meaningless addition to the problem of the roads and the rules, which are real and not man-made.

Wisdom observed that if old tales were true and if a human could pass on to another place, a backward glance would show that the long roads of desire he had come by were "plain in all their winding." Wisdom then stated the theme of *Pilgrim's Regress:* "[W]hen he found, he would know what it was that he had sought."

Referring to Exodus 16 as the Stewards' old chronicles, Wisdom advised John never to be greedy about his vision of the Island. He also helped John to avoid doubting that the thing he longed for was something real. "[W]hat you desire is no state

passage in poetic form. "Through this and through no other fault we fell, / Nor, being fallen, bear other pain than this, / —Always without hope in desire to dwell" (canto 4, lines 40–42).

of yourself at all, but something, for that very reason, Other and Outer." But Wisdom assured John that he must abandon hope for attainment, and wanting is better than having.

## 10

### WISDOM—ESOTERIC

*Secret Sustenance of Seemingly Austere Idealists*

Wanting may be better than having, but that night John had reason to wonder. The day had been warm and lazy, full of butterflies and quiet conversation.

During the night John was called out to play in the moonlight with sons and daughters of Wisdom. They were abnormally free from physical as well as emotional gravity. (Lewis was no doubt familiar with *The Light Princess* by George MacDonald, in which a girl was abnormally free from both kinds of gravity.) The playful people were leaping about like fleas on a food tray used for an arena. (The word *salver* means food tray. In most printings before 1980 the word *arena* was misprinted as *arema*.) Then they feasted on all kinds of things that would be forbidden in their home, even including hashish from a woman of the southern night and claret wine from Mother Kirk.

Karl (Marx, 1818–1883) offered brandy made by Savage's dwarfs. (Marx believed history's class struggle would lead to a violent overthrow of capitalism, producing a classless society. A temporary totalitarian dictatorship would bring about perfection in human relations.) Herbert (Spencer, 1820–1903) recommended Darwinian Claptrap food. (Spencer coined the phrase "survival of the fittest." He believed that societies were subject to the same laws of natural selection as plants and animals.) Benedict (Spinoza, 1632–1677) wanted a morsel of Judaism. (Spinoza contributed to seventeenth-century rationalism.)

For further adventures, Karl headed North to the Dwarfs, and Rudolph (Steiner, 1861–1925) headed South to the magicians. (Steiner was the first leader of the occult German Theosophic Association and later founded the Anthroposophical Society, which Lewis's friend Owen Barfield embraced.) Immanuel (Kant, 1724–1804) advised Rudolph that going to Puritania would be far better than going to the southern magicians. (In *Critique of Pure Reason* Kant argued that we know only what we gather from our senses.) Immanuel was accused of almost heading toward Mother Kirk, and Bernard (Bosanquet, 1848–1923) did just that. (Bosanquet was a British idealist.) The party disintegrated into scattered frivolity and fun.

In chapter 10 Lewis himself was in a playful mood, because he had John tumble down at the foot of a hawthorn bush when the midnight picnic began. Few readers are apt to notice Lewis's hint; he was referring to Nathaniel Hawthorne's "Young Goodman Brown" (1835). In that story a young man in Salem, Massachusetts, ventured into the woods one night to join a satanic cult. He was horrified to discover many virtuous fellow citizens already there, including Faith, his beloved bride. When he called out desperately to Faith, she and the rest of the coven disappeared.

Professor John G. West Jr. has pointed out that Lewis most likely read "The Celestial Railroad" by Hawthorne (1843), a satire based on Bunyan's *Pilgrim's Progress*. Like *Pilgrim's Regress,* "Celestial Railroad" launches an all-out attack on modern philosophy and modern religion. Its premise is that a railroad has been built to take pilgrims to the celestial city's very door, eliminating the need for a strenuous journey on foot. No more sweat, no more tears; pilgrims could sit back and enjoy the ride.

Some of Hawthorne's characters are Mr. Smooth-it-away, Rev. Mr. Shallow-deep, Rev. Mr. This-to-day, Rev. Mr. That-to-morrow, and Rev. Mr. Bewilderment. Giant Transcendentalist, like Bunyan's Giant Despair, is a forerunner of Lewis's Spirit of the Age: "a German by birth . . . but as to his form, his features, his substance, and his nature generally, it is the chief peculiarity of this huge miscreant that neither he for himself, nor anybody for him, has ever been able to describe them."[7] He looked somewhat like an ill-proportioned figure, but more like a heap of fog and duskiness.

# 11

## MUM'S THE WORD

### *Denial That Idealists Need Secret Sustenance*

John, like Goodman Brown, never found any evidence later that the midnight escapade had taken place. Either he had been deluded by a dream, or else the community secret was very well kept. As Clyde Kilby once observed, idealistic philosophers borrowed, "apparently without knowing it, from sources they would not always care to acknowledge."[8]

---

7. Nathaniel Hawthorne, "The Celestial Railroad," in *The Portable Hawthorne*, ed. Malcolm Cowley (New York: Viking Press, 1969), 252–53.
8. Clyde S. Kilby, *The Christian World of C. S. Lewis* (Grand Rapids, Mich.: William B. Eerdmans Publishing, 1964), 35.

## 12

MORE WISDOM

*Absolute Idealism*

Wisdom gave John and Vertue their third and final lesson, and Vertue was far healthier by the end of it. The headline "John is taught that the finite self cannot enter the Noumenal World" means that he can only go so far as his rationality and senses can take him, although there is indeed more to reality.

Wisdom quoted Berkeley's phrase "[A]ll this choir of heaven and furniture of earth" from *The Principles of Human Knowledge*. Berkeley had said that all these things do not exist without a mind, and Wisdom used the term imagination instead. His words "I am the Imaginer: I am one of his imaginations" were an echo of Emerson's "I am the doubter and the doubt," which John would quote in the next chapter. Wisdom taught John that we are in a sense one with our impersonal source. (Lewis was to argue against impersonality of our source in 1944 in *Beyond Personality*.) At this point in his journey, John was as far as the *evangelium eternum*, or "eternal gospel," which is pantheism. But Wisdom knew and included Mother Kirk's account of reality, and he knew and included John's experience of desire. Wisdom was no fool. John had been learning basic Hegelianism.

"Whatever may be our personal judgment of absolute idealism as the definite world-view, its logic is admittedly compelling." This is the judgment of Hunter Mead in his book *Types and Problems of Philosophy*. Mead warns that once we consent to take the first friendly step with Bishop Berkeley way back in the eighteenth century, the absolutist has us body and soul.[9] Mead personally rejects idealism, but he claims that the most innocent flirtation with *esse is percipi* leads inexorably to the all-devouring embrace of the Absolute. ("Esse Is Percipi" was the title of chapter 3 in book 4, where Reason explained her first riddle to John.)

Mead explains with unusual clarity that if all existence is the expression of Absolute Spirit, and if this Absolute is thus the whole of reality, then our consciousness can be nothing other than its self-consciousness. History and our experience of history are the two halves of one universal process. They are the objective and subjective aspects of what is. The world-process has purpose because all that occurs works toward realization of the potentialities that are inherent in Spirit. Everything that happens actualizes some further possibility of the Absolute.

This extreme view is one of the two major poles of philosophical thought. The two poles are naturalism and idealism. The naturalist philosopher, sometimes called "tough-minded," sees the world-order as mechanical, mindless, and non-moral. The idealist philosopher sees the world-order as a moral structure with intelligent purpose, values, and ideals. Naturalism appeals to common sense and sense experience, which idealists call mere "appearances." The idealist depends upon logic, including moral logic, to penetrate appearances and touch the underlying reality. In this sense Reality can be capitalized. Our source and true selves are part of Reality.

Wisdom spoke of the conflict between the wishes of our mortal and apparent selves and the wishes of our real and eternal selves.

---

9. Hunter Mead, *Types and Problems of Philosophy* (New York: Holt, Rinehart & Winston, 1959), 64–69.

In the last chapter of *The Great Divorce* (1945) Lewis presents that idea in a vivid picture. He describes a great assembly of gigantic forms all motionless, in deepest silence, standing around a little silver table and looking at it forever. On the table are little figures like chessmen who go about their activities. These chessmen are people as they appear to one another in this world. But those who stand and watch are the immortal souls of those very men and women. The name of the silver table is Time.

Lewis occasionally discussed philosophy and religion with his Roman Catholic friend Dom Bede Griffiths. In 1936 he congratulated Griffiths for learning some Aristotle, and he expressed his disgust at the "Neo-Scholasticism" fad at Oxford. He stressed how temporary every philosophical movement is. He meant, he said, that we have no abiding city even in philosophy. All passes away except the Word. In his next sentence he said he wanted to read Griffiths' review of *Pilgrim's Regress,* which he referred to as "my little book." He explained that he had used Mother Kirk because *Christianity* is not a plausible name for a character. Many had misunderstood his intent, especially after his publisher ("I fear Mr. Sheed is a rascal") insinuated on the jacket that Lewis had left Anglican Protestantism for Catholicism.[10]

A few lines farther along in that letter, after assuring Griffiths that he prayed for him, Lewis made a remark that reflected Wisdom's teaching about the wishes of our real and eternal selves: Whatever can we imagine heaven to be but *unimpeded* obedience? To Lewis this meant love, peace, and beauty.

10. Lewis to Griffiths, 8 January 1936, C. S. Lewis Letters to Dom Bede Griffiths, vol. 1 (1931–1948), cat. no. 1–23, index no. 0001–0050, Marion E. Wade Center, Wheaton College, Wheaton, Ill.

BOOK EIGHT

# AT BAY

*Conversion to Theism*

Book 8, "At Bay," begins with John and Vertue at the house of Wisdom and ends with John in a hermit's cave on the cliffside. This book tells of John's precarious journey where his pantheism turns into theism. Over half the pages are given to the teachings of the ancient hermit History.

Characters in book 8 are John, Vertue-gone-mad, the Man, and History. History tells about Northerners, Shepherds, and Pagans.

## 1

TWO KINDS OF MONIST

*Vertue Deserts John*

Vertue and John reacted in opposite ways to the words of Wisdom. John suddenly saw everything engulfed in the goodness of the Spirit, and Vertue saw his mortal self as a defect in the perfect goodness of the Spirit. Thus they were both monists or pantheists, but John was an optimist and Vertue was a pessimist. John held Hegel's view that all that happens actualizes more of the Absolute, so all is good.

Vertue referred to Isaiah 64:6, that our righteousness is as filthy rags, and he headed toward self-torture, intending to sleep on thorns and eat sour blackthorn fruit. (John would encounter a figurative thorn instead.) In the language of flowers, blackthorn blossoms are the symbol of difficulties. Because friendship is such a source of comfort and nurture, Vertue broke off his friendship with John as an act of self-punishment.

# 2

## JOHN LED

### "A Man" Helps John on His Way

When the ascent became too steep for John, and Vertue had tried to kill him, John determined to go back down. He rested where the grass was the kind sheep love. (John needed a good shepherd to help him.) Then a mysterious stranger hailed him and hauled him up the cliff, warning him that he and Vertue must recover together. This seems to be the same person who rode by in a coach the night John began his journey. Lewis tells in the headline who the Man is, in case readers don't guess that he is Christ. Lewis was referring to the famous 1904 conversion experience of Sadhu Sundar Singh (1889–1929), an international evangelist who was highly esteemed by devout Anglicans in Oxford in the 1920s.[1]

---

1. In 1945 Lewis fictionalized Sundar Singh in chapter five of *That Hideous Strength*. See "Golden Chains of Coincidence: A C. S. Lewis Puzzle Solved and Mystery to Ponder" by Kathryn Lindskoog in *Mythlore* 58 (summer 1989): 21–24.

## 3

### JOHN FORGETS HIMSELF

*An Accidental Prayer*

"That fellow has left me in a nice fix," John observed, perched on a ledge halfway up the cliff. Trying to live by his new belief in the benign Spirit, he called out to *him* (not to himself) for help. He was horrified to realize that he had been calling out to the Landlord, which brought back the rules, the black hole, and slavery. So he assured himself that the Landlord was only a figure of speech and could do him no harm.

## 4

### JOHN FINDS HIS VOICE

*His Absolute Becomes God*

John could only move along the ledge by praying to that part of the Spirit that was not a part of himself. So his pantheism turned into theism because he knew that he was not all one with the Spirit. John sang for the first time, a poem now titled "Footnote to All Prayers" in *Poems*.[2] It mentions Phidias, the greatest artist of ancient Greece, whose portrayal of the god Zeus in stone was one of the seven wonders of the ancient world. So all men who pray must depict God inaccurately. John was frightened by the meaning of his song.

---

2. C. S. Lewis, *Poems,* ed. Walter Hooper (New York: Harcourt Brace Jovanovich, Harvest, 1977), 129. (John's song has been heavily edited in *Poems;* the wording in *Pilgrim's Regress* is far more authoritative.)

## 5

### FOOD AT A COST

*Christ Provides for John*

A Man came to give John bread and water in the darkness. He advised John that if God can help, he can also command; that if he can respond to a call, he can also initiate. So in some sense John had a Landlord after all. John explained that he would rather operate on himself than submit to a surgeon, and the Man laughed kindly at John's apt imagery. A surgery was needed. Vertue had said when he entered the story, "The great thing is to do one's thirty miles a day." Now Christ said, in contrast, "[T]he great thing is to get the thorn out."

## 6

### CAUGHT

*John Gives in to God*

The bread had a familiar flat taste, which probably reminds readers of the unleavened bread of Passover or of Communion wafers. The Man's words lay like a cold weight that John must some day take up and carry, which reminds readers of Lewis's "Weight of Glory" essay and the cross itself. John went to sleep in stages but awakened with a start, his world filled with an unwelcome God and devoid of privacy.

John composed the song that is titled "Caught" in *Poems*.[3] He realized that what he had feared even before he met his brown girl had finally come true. "[I]f I go a new way I shall

3. Ibid., 115–16.

not be able to insist: I shall just have to take what comes." John saw that he would have to give up the Island and settle for the Landlord. His only hope was that the Landlord was less like the familiar concepts of his childhood and more like the obscure Absolute of philosophy.

# 7

## THE HERMIT

### *History Explains Northerners to John*

Once again, John entered a cave where he would be instructed in the proper way to see reality. When this happened before, he was imprisoned in a cave by the deceptive Spirit of the Age. This time he was a guest in the cave of the ancient hermit named History. John confided to History, "It seems to me, Father, that I am going where I do not wish; for I set out to find an Island and I have found a Landlord instead." So it seems indeed.

History told John that just as the Clevers rented from Mammon, and Mammon from the giant, and the giant from the Enemy, so the pale men rented from Ignorantia (ignorance) and Superbia (pride), daughters of the Enemy. Stoics, Manichees, Sparitates, and other counter-Romantics had lived on the Tableland also, all observing wasteful and destructive customs because of their wealth and extreme ignorance.

People who have read *Purgatory,* the second book of Dante's *Divine Comedy,* are apt to notice a resemblance between Lewis's ancient hermit and the ancient man who greeted and advised Dante when he began his ascent toward heaven.[4] Part of

4. Dante Alighieri, *Purgatory*, canto 1, lines 31–39.

Dante's symbolism in that passage meant that one who is oriented toward heaven becomes responsive to heaven's will rather than to the demands of human virtue. (This does not mean that there is any conflict between the two.)

Canto 1 of Dante's *Purgatory* also mentions sweet grass, subtly suggesting the Twenty-third Psalm, "He makes me lie down in green pastures."[5] Later in canto 3 Dante likens a group of wandering souls to a flock of sheep.[6] In book 8 of *Pilgrim's Regress* Lewis mentions "finer and shorter" grass. Twenty years after *Pilgrim's Regress*, in *The Horse and His Boy*, Lewis tells of another place with "the finest grass," home of another wise old hermit whose beard fell almost to his knees.[7] In all three of these accounts, a pilgrim (Dante, John, and Shasta) is entering a crucial new part of his spiritual journey.

# 8

## HISTORY'S WORDS

### The Story of the Shepherds and Pagans

Early in chapter 8 John complained that he did not know how to fit things together. History advised him about how Rules and pictures (morality and mythology) are meant to fit together. The Landlord used both, and they worked best together. Furthermore, Pagans (non-Jews) and Shepherds (Jews) were meant to be fit together, and they were so joined by the Landlord's Son. History quoted the Landlord's Son concerning the feet being set right first, referring to John 13:7–17; then "the hands and the head will come right sooner or later."

5. Ibid., canto 1, lines 124–129; Psalm 23:2 NRSV.
6. Dante, *Purgatory*, canto 3, lines 79–93.
7. C. S. Lewis, *The Horse and His Boy* (New York: Macmillan, 1954), chap. 10, p. 124.

John's feet had been set (by Christ) on the path that forced him to the hermit, who then worked at setting his head right.

Likewise, both John with his wants (sweet desire) and Vertue with his choice (conscience) needed to be fit together in order to be healthy. History told John that Vertue's father was Nomos, the Jewish Law. The one who reconciled the Shepherds and the Pagans, the Landlord's Son, was the only one who could reconcile John and Vertue.

Lewis's imagery reminds readers that quite literally it was Hebrew shepherds and pagan wise men who came to visit the infant Christ, and that the early church was soon made up of both Jews and pagans.

# 9

## MATTER OF FACT

### The Island and Other Forms of Desire

Jews began at the right end, morality, and Pagans began at the wrong end, the desire born of pictures; but it is all right to begin at the wrong end. Those who preached against the desire born of pictures were friends of the Enemy. Almost a year before Lewis wrote *Pilgrim's Regress* he said in a letter to Arthur Greeves that "Pagan stories are God expressing Himself through the minds of poets, using such images as He found there, while Christianity is God expressing Himself through what we call 'real things.' "[8]

The pictures used by the Landlord have varied through the ages, but each one is the arrival of some slightly unclear mes-

---

8. Lewis to Greeves, 18 October 1931, *They Stand Together: The Letters of C. S. Lewis to Arthur Greeves (1914–1963)*, ed. Walter Hooper (New York: Macmillan, 1979), 427.

sage that awakens desire and makes men long for something East or West of the world. This thing can be possessed, if at all, only in the act of desiring it. It is lost so quickly that the craving itself becomes craved. This something tends to be confused with common or even vile satisfactions that lie close at hand. Yet it is able, if anyone faithfully lives through a succession of attempts to attain it, to lead that person at last to where true joys are found. This is the "dialectic of desire."[9]

According to History, the strangest shape that the Landlord's message ever took was in the courtly love idea of the Middle Ages, which culminated in Dante's *Divine Comedy*. And the latest form of the Landlord's message was the early nineteenth-century Romantic love of nature, which came at about the time of the industrial revolution when desire was weak. Although these messages are imperfect, they nourish thousands of souls for thousands of years. When one form of the message dies, it is revived more fully in the heart of the next. The message comes in forms of desire.

In 1954 Lewis wrote to his old friend Bede Griffiths that he was convinced that all joy, as distinct from mere pleasure or amusement, emphasizes our pilgrim status. Joy "always reminds, beckons, awakens desire. Our best havings are wantings."[10] "Clopinel" refers to Jean de Meung of the thirteenth century, and "Medium Aevum" is Middle Ages.

---

9. C. S. Lewis, *Surprised by Joy: The Shape of My Early Life* (San Diego: Harcourt Brace Jovanovich, Harvest, 1966), chap. 14, p. 219. See also C. S. Lewis, "Afterword to Third Edition," *The Pilgrim's Regress,* deluxe illustrated edition (Grand Rapids, Mich.: William B. Eerdmans Publishing, 1981), 205 (p. 10 in preface to 1943 edition).
10. Lewis to Griffiths, 5 November 1954, *Letters of C. S. Lewis,* edited and with a memoir by W. H. Lewis, revised and enlarged edition edited by Walter Hooper (San Diego: Harcourt, Brace & Co., Harvest, 1993), 441.

## 10

### ARCHTYPE AND ECTYPE

*The Source and Fruit of Desire*

At the end of book 8 Lewis mentioned again that he was dreaming the story, and at this point John was on the borders of sleep. The hermit's song John heard then has been titled "The Naked Seed" by the editor of *Poems*.[11] In this prayer the hermit sang of dry times when a person has no right thoughts at all and feels no desires at all, and the soul seems to have died. Then Christ, who never wearies, can think for us and desire for us, and keep us alive until we awaken.

---

11. Lewis, *Poems*, 117. (This poem might have been better titled "Night Song of the Hermit" or "Keep Watch for Me.")

BOOK NINE

# ACROSS THE CANYON

*Conversion to Christianity*

Book 9, "Across the Canyon," is largely about seeing, from the first sentence to the last. Furthermore, in the first chapter and the last, John sees the Island as the Landlord's castle. Between these two sightings he is forced to confront his deeply repressed fear of death, to cast himself into Christianity, to travel to the western end of the world, and to accept an angelic guide who strengthens his vision.

Characters include John, Contemplation, Reason, Death, Mother Kirk, Vertue, eight wraiths, a great company of pilgrims, and Slikisteinsauga (Sleekstone Eyes).

# 1

### ACROSS THE CANYON BY THE INNER LIGHT

### *A View of the Island as the Landlord's Castle*

The very first phrase in book 9 is "When John opened his eyes," and that is what the rest of book 9 and even book 10 is about.

When John went to sleep in the house of Wisdom, he went "Across the Canyon by Moonlight." In contrast, he went to sleep in History's cave and went "Across the Canyon by the Inner Light." Both trips were in dreams, but the first trip was illusion and the second trip was true.

Chapter 1 is awash with both light and water. Contemplation lit up the cave, and John followed her out into the black rain. The two of them moved in a sphere of light, filled with bright and iridescent raindrops. They crossed the canyon and crossed the sea, and then their "drop of light" merged into an "ocean of light." Dew soaked their feet and light ran down as a river. Gradual realization of where he was spread circles of dismay in "the pool" of John's mind. John was beyond the brook. After being drenched with light, John was still so terrified of the black hole that he screamed and escaped.

# 2

### THIS SIDE BY LIGHTNING

### *Reason Forces John on His Way*

After his bright dream, John returned to deep darkness and saw with his inner eye the black hole, his precarious ledge, himself falling down the dark crags, and Uncle George's terrible face. By lightning John saw Reason, sword drawn, blocking his retreat and forcing him on beyond the cave. He realized that if he could cast Reason down, he too would be destroyed. Reason forced him on to where he beheld something dreadful by moonlight.

# 3

## THIS SIDE BY THE DARKNESS

### *John Accepts Dying*

What appeared to John was Death, who claimed to be more terrible than the black hole. Referring to Isaiah 30:10, Death stated, "They have prophesied soft things to you," and claimed that the idea of death as nonexistence is a false comfort. John had repressed the memory of Uncle George's face for a long time; at last he had to look at it again. Furthermore, he learned that a large part of dying is the "being blindfolded." John had only the choice between utter helplessness and utter risk. He chose the risk. By so choosing to lay down his liberty to Death, John was cured of the terror of it. Next he looked and saw where he must go—down to a group of people by water at the bottom of the chasm.

When the stranger had told John, "[T]he great thing is to get the thorn out," the words had lain in John's heart "like a cold weight that he must some day take up and carry." Now he descended the cliff with a cold, leaden fear which seemed to be that weight. The descent reminds readers of Gerard Manley Hopkins' lines with which Lewis was no doubt familiar:

O the mind, mind has mountains; cliffs of fall
Frightful, sheer, no-man-fathomed. Hold them cheap
May who ne'er hung there.[1]

## 4

### SECURUS TE PROJICE

*John Surrenders to Christianity*

The title of chapter 4 means "Throw yourself down confidently," from St. Augustine; the first sentence calls the floor of the canyon the floor of *Peccatum Adae*, the Sin of Adam. John approached in defeat, because Mother Kirk had nothing he desired.

Describing his long search in a poem once, Lewis told in six short stanzas how he had to "give himself up" and meet the object he hunted in the appointed place where *He* hunts. Not in nature, or in man—but in one Particular Man, with a specific height and weight and trade, speaking Aramaic. That poem, "No Beauty We Could Desire," is available in Lewis's *Poems*.[2]

Mother Kirk's response is the theme of the entire book to this point: "You have come a long way round to reach this place, whither I would have carried you in a few moments. But it is very well." The last comment echoes the words Christ spoke in a vision to Lady Julian of Norwich in the fifteenth century: "But all shall be well and all shall be well, and

---

1. Gerard Manley Hopkins, "No worst, there is none," *Poems and Prose of Gerard Manley Hopkins*, ed. W. H. Gardner (Harmondsworth, Middlesex, England: Penguin Books, 1968), 61.
2. *Poems,* ed. Walter Hooper (New York: Harcourt Brace Jovanovich, Harvest, 1977), 124.

all manner of thing shall be well."³ At last John was willing to listen to Mother Kirk tell him what to do.

In the spring of 1930 Lewis had been rereading George MacDonald's fairy stories and might have reread *The Golden Key*, which included this favorite passage of his: "The Old Man of the Earth stooped over the floor of the cave, raised a huge stone from it, and left it leaning. It disclosed a great hole that went plumb-down. 'That is the way,' he said.

"'But there are no stairs.'

"'You must throw yourself in. There is no other way.'"⁴

In the summer of 1930 Lewis and his friend Owen Barfield were swimming naked in the small Thame (not Thames) river out in the country; Lewis finally learned to dive, which meant a great change in his life, with "important (religious) connections."⁵ He stated in a letter to Arthur Greeves that he was not graceful, but that he did get in head first. Three weeks later, Lewis wrote prophetically to Greeves that "[i]t is an interesting and rather grim enquiry how much of our present selves we could hope to take with us if there were another life."⁶ Lewis assumed that anything merely intellectual or theoretical must be lost to us when we die because it is probably dependent upon the physical brain. He suspected that only what has gone into our very depths could pass on to the next life. If so, our religious thinking may come to nothing in the end, and only the religion we practice is likely to go with us. This is the kind of required stripping away of ragged clothes

---

3. Lady Julian of Norwich, *Revelations of Divine Love* (New York: Harper & Bros., 1961), 42.
4. George MacDonald, *The Golden Key and Other Stories* (Grand Rapids, Mich.: William B. Eerdmans Publishing, 1989), 26–27.
5. Lewis to Greeves, 8 July 1930, *They Stand Together: The Letters of C. S. Lewis to Arthur Greeves (1914–1963)*, ed. Walter Hooper (New York: Macmillan, 1979), 369.
6. Lewis to Greeves, 29 July 1930, *They Stand Together*, 370.

which left John naked at the edge of the water.

Next, the wraiths of eight of John's friends and enemies came to advise John not to take the plunge. Notably absent were Wisdom, Reason, and the pale Mr. Angular. That was Lewis's tribute to them.

# 5

## ACROSS THE CANYON

### John Comes to the End of the World

Lewis's dream was dark as John swam through an underground tunnel and then climbed through underground caves learning mysteries. This passage has reminded some readers of the underground passage in Lewis's *Perelandra* (1943). Here Wisdom came to trouble John, claiming that these adventures were only mythology. But then the voice of God spoke to John. The voice mentioned Semele, who was a mortal girl accidentally burned to death when Zeus appeared in order to love her without his being veiled. One of the most frequently quoted sentences from *Pilgrim's Regress* is "For this end I made your senses and for this end your imagination, that you might see My face and live." The voice has spoken to John six times in this book, and this final time it says the most. (These manifestations of the voice were in book 1, chapters 2, 4, and 6; book 8, chapters 2 and 5; and book 9, chapter 5.)

In the last year of his life, Lewis published the following sentence in an article in the American periodical *Show:* "[Y]ou may come (some do) to believe that that voice . . .

which speaks in your conscience and in some of your intensest joys, which is sometimes so obstinately silent, sometimes so easily silenced, and then at other times so loud and emphatic, is in fact the closest contact you have with the mystery; and therefore finally to be trusted, obeyed, feared and desired more than all other things." This article, "The Seeing Eye," is available in *Christian Reflections*. A misprint there has made it seem to say "[T]hat voice which speaks *is* [italics added] your conscience," but Lewis wrote "[T]hat voice which speaks *in* [italics added] your conscience."[7]

After the message from God in the caverns, John emerged; and Lewis tells how his own dreaming eyes were full of light and color and how he watched and what he saw. Then John saw the Island. Thousands looked with him. The longing was humbler and less wild than ever before; and to John this began to seem well.

## 6

### NELLA SUA VOLUNTADE

### *John's Eyes Are Sharpened*

The title of chapter 6 means "In His Will" and refers to "In His will is our peace" from *Paradise*, the third and last book of Dante's *Divine Comedy*.[8]

Lewis did not see what happened to the other pilgrims, but Slikisteinsauga, one of the Landlord's mountain children,

---

7. C. S. Lewis, "The Seeing Eye," in *Christian Reflections,* ed. Walter Hooper (Grand Rapids, Mich.: William B. Eerdmans Publishing, 1967), 170. This essay was originally published in *Show* 3 (February 1963) under the unfortunate title "Onward Christian Spacemen."
8. Dante Alighieri, *Paradise,* canto 3, line 85.

came to guide John and Vertue and to sharpen their eyesight by his very company. (A sleekstone is a stone used to polish something else.) Sure enough, the first thing he asked them to do was to look at the Island more carefully, and John said simply, "I see." He saw there the shape of the eastern mountains.

John wondered how traveling West could have led him toward the eastern mountains, and the Guide answered, "[T]he world is round." In 1940 Lewis began a poem with "Naked apples, woolly-coated peaches / Swelled on the garden wall" and ended it with "The world is round." To emphasize his point, he titled the poem "The World Is Round." This little-known poem, published in the wartime anthology *Fear No More* from Cambridge University Press, hints at hope for a future return to the Garden of Eden after the long, painful journey of fallen human life and the black frost of the war.[9] In biblical terms, the message of that poem and *Pilgrim's Regress* is that of Genesis 50:19–20. God can use evil for good.

Slikisteinsauga summed up the story of John's life when he told him that the Landlord had brought him the shortest way, although there was no question that the journey would look odd on a map.

---

9. C. S. Lewis, "The World Is Round," in *Fear No More: A Book of Poems for the Present Time by Living English Poets* (Cambridge: Cambridge University Press, 1940), 85. The editor of *Poems* (1977) changed the poem's title to "Poem for Psychoanalysts and/or Theologians" and published a revised version of the poem itself.

BOOK TEN

# THE REGRESS

*Journey to the Brook of Death*

Book 10, "The Regress," starts at the western end (beginning) of the world and finishes at the brook at the edge of the eastern mountains. After the color and triumph of book 9, book 10 is rather harsh. It stresses the severity of mercy. This part of the story was predicted in a casual sentence Lewis wrote to Greeves in 1930, where he said, "The road is always turning round and going back to places we seemed to have left—but they are *different* (yet in a way the same) when you come to them the second time."[1]

---

1. Lewis to Greeves, 31 June 1930, *They Stand Together: The Letters of C. S. Lewis to Arthur Greeves (1914–1963)*, ed. Walter Hooper (New York: Macmillan, 1979), 366.

## 1

### THE SAME YET DIFFERENT

*John's New View of the World*

Now John began the Christian life, in Lewis's dream, armed and guided by the angel. He saw the land as it really was, lying between sadism and masochism. John was appalled that life looked harder than ever, and the Guide quoted Shakespeare's Hecate in *Macbeth,* who said,

> And you all know security
> Is mortals' chiefest enemy.[2]

For the first time, Vertue sang. This poem appears under the title "Wormwood" in *Poems*.[3] Wormwood is the biblical name in Revelation 8:10–11 for Mother Kirk's land-grabber. Tenth hierarch means the one ruler outside the nine levels of heaven. Ahriman is the Persian "Prince of Evil." Heavenly love and evil's raging lust are the only alternatives; the rest is passing illusion. Any man who does not live as a clear window for the Father's light will be melted by Satan's burning heat. Vertue asked God not to open his eyes to this harsh reality too often.

## 2

### THE SYNTHETIC MAN

*Seeing through Sensible Worldliness*

It was Mr. Sensible who advised John to seek his own solid good, and Mr. Sensible turned out in the end to be invisible,

---

2. *Macbeth*, 3.5.32–33.
3. C. S. Lewis, *Poems,* ed. Walter Hooper (New York: Harcourt Brace Jovanovich, Harvest, 1977), 87.

he was so close to nothing. The Guide quoted Shakespeare again, calling Sensible a man of shreds and patches, which is what Hamlet called his deceptive uncle/stepfather just before the invisible ghost of Hamlet's murdered father manifested itself to him. Sensible's parting words had been "Do what you will," quoted from Rabelais. But Rabelais was referring to a great Steward of the olden days, Saint Augustine, who said *Habe caritatem et fac quod vis:* "Love, and do what you will," and Augustine was referring to Christ's words "'You shall love the Lord your God with all your heart, and with all your soul, and with all your mind.' This is the greatest and first commandment. And a second is like it: 'You shall love your neighbor as yourself.' On these two commandments hang all the law and the prophets" (Matt. 22:37–40 NRSV). Mr. Sensible had never sensed reality. He had been extremely *insensible,* which is part of Lewis's wordplay.

# 3

## LIMBO

### *Seeing Philosophy's Doom*

The Guide showed John that the Valley of Wisdom is really an island in a swamp area of hell, a place of twilight and sighing near the black hole. It is the Limbo described by Dante, where men are doomed "to be cut off from all hope, yet live on in desire."[4]

God mercifully keeps the hopeless desire of those in Limbo from becoming corrupted by evil, and so certain pure-

---

4. Dante Alighieri, *Hell,* canto 4, line 42 (unpublished version by Kathryn Lindskoog). See also *Surprised by Joy: The Shape of My Early Life* (San Diego: Harcourt Brace Jovanovich, Harvest, 1966), chap. 13, p. 210.

minded philosophers do not fall into the depths of Hell. Both the angelic Guide and John understood that the pain of their unfulfilled desire (for the blessedness they were made for) was far better than a lack of that desire. But the angelic Guide told John, "[Y]ou understand it already better than I can." Lewis wrote more than once about the contrasting human and angelic (purely spiritual) modes of knowing truth. In 1946 Lewis published "On Being Human" in *Punch*. In that poem Lewis contrasted the transcendent consciousness of angels with "[t]he pleasure and the pang" of human consciousness, confined as it is inside the tiny "parlour of the brain."[5] Unlike angels, the Maker has shared our human consciousness.

When the Guide added, "Men say that his love and his wrath are one thing," Lewis might have been referring to a saying of George MacDonald's that he valued, "The terror of God is but the other side of His love."[6]

The Guide's first song was about mercy, but the editor of *Poems* titled it "Divine Justice."[7] It is a perfect triolet. (A triolet is an eight-line poem with rhyme scheme abaaabab. Line one is identical with four and seven, and line two is identical with line eight.) As in Vertue's song where Wormwood was bound in the dark seven-walled furnace of Self, in the Guide's song hell itself is bound and contained eternally.

---

5. "On Being Human," *Punch*, 8 May 1946, 402. A revised version appears in *Poems* (1977).
6. C. S. Lewis, ed., *George MacDonald: 365 Readings* (New York: Macmillan, 1947), 38.
7. Lewis, *Poems*, 98. "In His Mercy" might have been a better title for this poem.

## 4

### THE BLACK HOLE

*Understanding Hell*

The Guide explained how eating wild mountain apples in spite of the Landlord's warning created in man a permanently worm-eaten will, which made a blackness that would spread and multiply itself (fissiparous) eternally if not bound by (Aristotle's) form and limit. So the Landlord restricted the blackness of lost souls to what is like a hole in reality. It was the best he could do for them, once they could not be cured.

The editor of *Poems* titled the Guide's second song "Nearly They Stood."[8] The first stanza tells how all lost souls could have been saved by a mere shadow of turning at a crucial point. The second stanza tells how those who were saved could have been lost by a shift in choice as slender as strands of a spider web. In the third stanza Lewis warns himself not to carelessly step past the rivulet the width of a hair which would bar him forever from salvation.

## 5

### SUPERBIA

*Seeing the Ugly Pride of Scrupulosity*

In contrast to the kind of scrupulosity expressed in the song titled "Nearly They Stood," which was about choices and destiny, the travelers soon encountered a personification of the scrupulosity that is a kind of spiritual pride.

---

8. Ibid., 102–3. "The Choice of Way" might be a more accurate title.

History had told John that the tableland was owned by Superbia, and now they saw her and heard her song.[9] The first stanza tells how Pride reduced her land to sterile stone. The second stanza tells how she reduced her body to a dry skeleton. And the third stanza tells how she reduced her soul to frozen steel. The disgusting helot described in lines 2–6 was a female serf in ancient Sparta. The monad in the last line was an elementary spiritual quality supposedly above sin and grace.

Because Vertue felt there was some merit in Superbia's insane distaste for the organic, the Guide quoted from *The Book of Common Prayer* about the birth of the Landlord's Son: "When thou tookest upon thee to deliver man thou didst humble thyself to be born of a Virgin." The Guide endorsed Mary's motherhood and all it represents, including matter itself.

When the Guide concluded that few human jokes have any point in the Landlord's presence, he meant that when there is no embarrassment or distaste at all concerning bodily functions, jokes about sex and other awkward topics such as elimination fall flat. Their impact depends upon at least a little discomfort in the listener. The Landlord isn't "decent" enough to feel at all uncomfortable about human bodies. It is notable that in a letter written to Greeves, Lewis admitted his tendency toward physical disgust in response to news of the birth of a calf. His revulsion rather puzzled him. He said he realized that "God is gross and never heard of decency and cares nothing for refinement."[10]

Next Vertue sang a song that is called "Posturing" in *Poems*.[11] Vertue claimed that he could easily have starved

---

9. Ibid., 88. The editor gave the song of Superbia the title "Virtue's Independence." "Pride's Sterility," "Once Filthy," or "Scraped Clean" might have been more accurate titles.
10. Lewis to Greeves, 29 July 1930, *They Stand Together*, 371.
11. Lewis, *Poems*, 89. It could well be titled "The End of Pride."

while admiring himself in the mirror, letting good food go to waste. But he glimpsed his ugliness. Then he saw that in comparison to his Creator his own beauty was foul. Pure Love can turn disillusioned Self-Love into humility.

## 6

### IGNORANTIA

*Seeing the Ignorance of Technological Society*

Lewis explains that he only remembers snatches of the conversation in his dream. He recalls talk of how the northern people were overemphasizing mechanical knowledge and suppressing classical education, thus greatly increasing ignorance. Lewis's Guide may have been mistaken about the limited destructive potential of modern armaments, but much of his jaundiced view of the benefits of technology proved true in the first sixty years following the publication of *Pilgrim's Regress*.

The Guide's third song was entitled "Deception" by the editor of *Poems*.[12] The first stanza predicts increased technological destruction of natural (ecological) beauty, but ends with faith in the Resurrection. The second stanza predicts increased mental enslavement to false propaganda and ignorance, but ends with faith in God's ability to deliver his people from slavery. The third stanza predicts that people will consider the changes in the first two stanzas irrevocable, but ends with faith in the unchanging nature of God.

---

12. Ibid., 90. "Changes" or "Irrevocability" might fit better.

# 7

## LUXURIA

### *Seeing the Evil of Sexual Indulgence*

The title of this chapter, "Luxuria," refers to the old classification of the Seven Deadly Sins and means "unchastity."[13] (The Bantam edition of the *Regress* mistakenly footnotes luxuria as "luxury".) John saw victims of lust melting off into many snakes, yet remaining selves, in a horrifying scene reminiscent of canto 25 in Dante's *Inferno*. The tenth poem in *Pilgrim's Regress* is the anguished prayer of a young man racked by extreme temptation, begging God to rescue him. The editor of *Poems* calls this poem "Forbidden Pleasure."[14]

Right after his cry to God for help, the addict succumbed and drank the witch's poison and was lost. Then the witch tempted John himself with five methods. First, she freely admitted that this drink would not quench thirst long, but she urged him to sip it anyway for his great thirst. Second, she emphasized that he was very thirsty and that he could not be sure which drink would prove fatal. Third, she claimed that he was too weak to resist her this time, but that in the future he could probably resist her. Fourth, she said that there was no other pleasure ahead, so he was bound to give in eventually and might as well get it over with. Fifth, she discouraged him by wearying him with her persistence.

The eleventh poem in *Pilgrim's Regress* was composed by John. The editor of *Poems* called it "Lilith" (a female demon

---

13. Lewis to Greeves, 30 January 1930, *They Stand Together*, 342. In this letter to Arthur Greeves, Lewis lists each of the Seven Deadly Sins, translates them, and comments upon them.
14. Lewis, *Poems*, 116. "The Struggle" or "Festering Fire" would be more fitting.

in Jewish legend).[15] The ultimate form of sexual temptation is an apparent emptiness and bleakness in the rest of life, for which sex is anodyne or painkiller. Lewis had written this poem in April 1930 and sent it to Greeves then, explaining that sometimes we fall into sexual sin because the temptation makes everything else seem so drab—although the temptation itself is not very attractive.[16] Resisting sexual temptation drained John greatly; he was exhausted.

# 8

## THE NORTHERN DRAGON

### *John Wins Endurance*

John had to fight the northern dragon of rigidity, greed, and coldness. There was only one such dragon left, because *serpens nisi serpentem comederit* (it is not a serpent if it doesn't eat serpents). John overheard the dragon croaking a poem, the twelfth in *Pilgrim's Regress*. The editor of *Poems* called this one "The Dragon Speaks."[17] The dragon recalled how it had hatched from a snake's egg ("worm" used to mean snake) and had mated ("druery" means lovemaking). By eating his wife, he had become a dragon. John was somewhat enchanted by the dragon's self-pitying song of greed and miserliness. But when it tried to crush him in its icy grip, he stabbed it to death, gaining tremendous strength and freeing himself forever from panic and greed.

---

15. Ibid., 95. "Witch's Wine" or "Anodyne" might be more fitting.
16. Lewis to Greeves, 29 April 1930, *They Stand Together*, 353.
17. Lewis, *Poems*, 92–93. "The Dragon's Song" would be more accurate. Two-thirds of the lines of this poem were altered in *Poems*, and not for the better. The version in *Pilgrim's Regress* is far more authoritative.

## 9

### THE SOUTHERN DRAGON

*Vertue Wins Passion*

In chapter 5, "Superbia," Vertue had felt "there is something foul about all these natural processes." The Guide had warned him not to be too dainty, and he had answered, "Well, . . . I will think this over." In chapter 9, Vertue's victory over the southern dragon of unprincipled intoxication was even more dramatic than John's victory in chapter 8. The fact that hot but harmless flame was on Vertue and that he reeled like a drunk man made his victory reminiscent of Pentecost.

Vertue's victory chant appears in *Poems* under the title "Dragon-Slayer."[18] He had met the dragon near a shaw (small wood). The dragon's hot spew (vomit) worked against it as Vertue and his sword incorporated the heat. When Vertue sank his teeth into the dead beast's heart he became intoxicated for the first time, exulting over nature (Behemoth and Leviathan are huge animals referred to in Job 3:8 and 40:15) and singing "I shall rise again" and *"Io Paean,"* a traditional Greek shout of triumph and praise.

## 10

### THE BROOK

*Affirmation of Our Mode of Knowing and Loving*

The first paragraph of chapter 10 is the happiest part of *Pilgrim's Regress*. For the first time, John and Vertue were

---
18. Ibid., 94.

mature enough to indulge in childlike laughing and dancing and singing. This scene is a bit like the joyful ending of James Stephens' *Crock of Gold*:

> And they took the Philosopher from his prison, and even the Intellect of Man they took from the hands of the doctors and lawyers, from the sly priests, from the professors whose mouths are gorged with sawdust, and the merchants who sell blades of grass—the awful people of Fomor . . . and then they returned again, dancing and singing to the country of the gods.[19]

Lewis first read this witty book-length adult fairy tale shortly after its publication in 1912, and it remained a favorite for the rest of his life.

As Lewis put it, at this point his dream was full of light and noise. John was neither fearful nor questioning. But once more, for the last time, he wept.

John was back at book 1, chapter 1, in a sense; but it was too late for him to communicate with his dead parents. The Guide led John and Vertue to the brook; they had died to many things in their journey, but now they were going to die in earnest. Book 10 is unique, not least because the desire for Joy was forgotten and life's goal had become the object of the Joy instead.

Vertue, having gained emotions, finally experienced sadness. The editor called his song about death "When the Curtain's Down" in *Poems*.[20] Vertue saw each man as a unique blending of body and spirit which will be eternally unmade at death. Only Christ is resurrected. Vertue quoted from "Gloria in Excelsis" in *The Book of Common Prayer*: "Thou only

---

19. James Stephens, *The Crock of Gold* (New York: Macmillan, 1935), 298.
20. Lewis, *Poems*, 97. "Never Restored" may be a better title.

art holy; Thou only art the Lord." Vertue attributed to God the figurative wings of the Egyptian god of the dead, which enfold the past. God's scepter includes the power of communication with the dead, and they live on only in God's consciousness. This was Vertue's idea, not John's—nor Lewis's.

John corrected Vertue: "Be sure it is not for nothing that the Landlord has knit our hearts so closely to time and place—to one friend rather than another and one shire more than all the land." Lewis expressed this insight vividly in one of the most evocative and heartfelt poems he ever wrote, "Your True Antiquities." There, in sixteen lines, Lewis relates his adult knowledge of the history of the world (from the Garden of Eden to Schliemann's discovery of Troy) to his early childhood home in Ireland: the lawn, the clump of trees, and some odds and ends in the attic.[21] Lewis uses the intense nostalgia of his own childhood memories to illustrate the nature of human cognition and, by implication, the nature of human affections.

The crucial fifteenth poem in *Pilgrim's Regress* was altered and titled "Scazons" by the editor of *Poems,* but the original

---

21. C. S. Lewis, *The Collected Poems of C. S. Lewis,* ed. Walter Hooper (London: HarperCollins, 1994), 250–52. The provenance of "Your True Antiquities" is mysterious. As belatedly published in 1994 in the midst of a long, rambling poem called "Finchley Avenue," the phrase "These are your true antiquities" merely refers to some "Tuddorish" homes that the writer happened to admire on a street overlooking London. But when lines 31–46 are extricated from their banal context, the phrase "These are your true antiquities" suddenly refers to what are in fact nostalgic scenes from Lewis's childhood home. Seen this way, "Your True Antiquities" is profoundly and personally Lewisian. Like a trick drawing in which a figure in plain view is not recognized because of its background, "Your True Antiquities" is not recognized in the midst of its inappropriate background. (In Gestalt psychology this phenomenon is referred to as "figure" [the focus of interest], "background" [the setting or context], and the "aha!" experience of delayed recognition.) Whatever the origin of mediocre "Finchley Avenue," "Your True Antiquities" is a profound poem, tightly written with exquisite tenderness, and it should be made available to Lewis readers everywhere.

version is better, and "Pang of the Particular" might be a better title.[22] John saw how a man's heart is especially bound to the local and the particular people and things in his own life. This is the crux of being human rather than pure spirit. Thus humans are a little higher than the angels, and humans are vulnerable to pain. The last stanza of this poem echoes an image in the second stanza of Lewis's unpublished *Odyssey*, begun a few months earlier: "Oh perfect life, unquivering, self-enkindled flame / From which my fading candle first was lit. . . ."[23] In contrast to quivering human flames, John observes, angels are as cold as the moon, merely reflecting God's light.

Then at last Lewis's dream darkened for the final time, and as he awakened he heard the three travelers singing as they crossed the brook and started up the mountain. The editor of *Poems* called their lyric "Angel's Song" but there are three songs of the angel in *Pilgrim's Regress*, and this one is uniquely ironic.[24] Slikisteinsauga laments that he can never know what loss means, and that he cannot experience sorrow. But for the pilgrims this final song is one of great joy and gratitude. For human pilgrims the cup called sorrow in the last stanza is the Eucharist.

*Pilgrim's Regress* was Lewis's first published fiction. In 1956 his last published fiction appeared: the mysterious novel *Till We Have Faces*, which became his favorite. He said that

---

22. Lewis, *Poems,* 118. This is the third poem from *The Pilgrim's Regress* to be revised without explanation in Lewis's posthumous *Poems,* edited by Walter Hooper in 1964. The three appear there as "Footnote to All Prayers" from book 8, chapter 4; "The Dragon Speaks" from book 10, chapter 8; and "Scazons" from book 10, chapter 10. At latest count, forty-five poems in that collection are actually revisions of poems published in Lewis's lifetime. The revisions are puzzling because none are explained, and many are clearly inferior to the originals.
23. See pages xxv–xxvi in the introduction of this book for details.
24. Lewis, *Poems,* 107. "The Cup" might have been an ideal title.

in a sense he had been working on it most of his life, and to some readers it seems like an extraordinary use of themes he first used in *Pilgrim's Regress*. Early in *Till We Have Faces* the heroine Psyche begs her heartbroken sister:

> Do you remember? The colour and the smell, and looking across at the Grey Mountain in the distance? And because it was so beautiful, it set me longing, always longing. Somewhere else there must be more of it. Everything seemed to be saying, Psyche come! But I couldn't (not yet) come and I didn't know where I was to come to. It almost hurt me. I felt like a bird in a cage when the other birds of its kind are flying home....
>
> ... I am going, you see, to the Mountain. You remember how we used to look and long? And all the stories of my gold and amber house, up there against the sky, where we thought we should never really go? The greatest King of all was going to build it for me. If only you could believe it, Sister!...
>
> ... my country, the place where I ought to have been born. Do you think it all meant nothing, all the longing? The longing for home? For indeed it now feels not like going, but like going back. All my life the god of the Mountain has been wooing me. Oh, look up once at least before the end and wish me joy. I am going to my lover.[25]

*Pilgrim's Regress* is a complex quest narrative that takes the traveler home. T. S. Eliot (1888–1965) summarized that kind of intellectual quest in "Little Gidding" from *Four Quartets* (1935–1942):

---

25. C. S. Lewis, *Till We Have Faces* (New York: Harcourt, Brace & Co., 1957), 74–76.

> We shall not cease from exploration
> And the end of all our exploring
> Will be to arrive where we started
> And know the place for the first time.[26]

Lewis could not have foreseen those famous lines from Eliot when he wrote *Pilgrim's Regress*. But he almost surely had in mind the following lines from "Hymn to God My God, in My Sickness" by the great poet John Donne (1572–1631):

> . . . As West and East
>   In all flat maps (and I am one) are one,
>   So death doth touch the resurrection.
>
> Is the Pacific Sea my home? Or are
>   The Eastern riches? Is Jerusalem? . . .
>   . . . . . . . . . . . . . . . . . .
>
> We think that Paradise and Calvary,
>   Christ's cross and Adam's tree, stood in one place;
>   Look, Lord, and find both Adams met in me.[27]

---

26. T. S. Eliot, "Little Gidding," *Four Quartets* (New York: Harcourt Brace Jovanovich, Harvest, 1971), 5.239–42.
27. John Donne, *John Donne's Poetry,* ed. Arthur Clements (New York: W. W. Norton & Co., 1992), 128–29.

APPENDIX ONE

# THE ESSENCE OF ALLEGORY

At the time when C. S. Lewis suddenly wrote *Pilgrim's Regress,* he had already started work on the scholarly book which was to assure him of permanent respect among historians of English literature, *The Allegory of Love* (1936). This is a study of the allegorical love poetry of the Middle Ages, and it was eight years from inception to publication. It seems fitting that Lewis wrote his own successful allegory in the midst of this study of allegory. He never returned to writing sustained allegory again, but he never stopped reading allegory.

As Lewis's friend Dorothy L. Sayers points out in the opening of her 1954 essay "The Writing and Reading of Allegory," in this century the term is frequently used as a pejorative, as in "'The book never degenerates into allegory, but is, on the contrary, a rich and evocative work of the imagination.' Or finally, the word may be applied, quite at random, to something that is not allegory at all, but which happens to contain some religious or moral teaching that the critic dislikes or fails to understand."[1]

1. Dorothy Sayers, "The Writing and Reading of Allegory," in *The Whimsical Christian: 18 Essays* (New York: Macmillan, 1978), 205.

Sayers cites C. S. Lewis's *Perelandra* as an example of the latter. Lewis prefaced *Perelandra* with the following disclaimer: "All the human characters in this book are purely fictitious, and none of them is allegorical."[2] Nevertheless, one reviewer described the book's opening and then dismissed the rest with "Then the allegory begins." Sayers observes that the reviewer is not worthy of further comment.

She continues,

> Now, when a whole department of literature is thus unanimously and, as it were, automatically condemned for the mere crime of being itself, and excluded from serious critical attention, it is pretty safe to say that we have simply forgotten how to judge it. It is extremely improbable, to say the least of it, that a genre that, in the past, produced such acknowledged masterpieces as *The Divine Comedy*, *The Faerie Queene*, and *The Pilgrim's Progress*, is altogether worthless. Neither is it probable that a genre that enjoyed so many hundreds of years of popularity corresponds to no fundamental need in human nature.[3]

Lewis explains in *The Allegory of Love* that an allegorist starts with an immaterial fact such as wrath and then invents a fictitious material object such as a person to depict wrath in his story.[4] The allegorist does this consciously and intentionally, never confusing the reality of wrath with the reality of his invented person. Lewis quotes Dante's observation in *Vita Nuova* that he wrote about love as if it were a physical being with intelligence of its own. "Now this, according to the

---

2. C. S. Lewis, preface to *Perelandra: A Novel* (New York: Macmillan, 1944).
3. Sayers, "Allegory," 206.
4. C. S. Lewis, *The Allegory of Love: A Study in Medieval Tradition* (London: Oxford University Press, 1936), 44–47.

truth," said Dante, "is false." Love is not a physical being, he explained, but is only a condition that occurs in a physical being. Allegorists know what they are doing, and it used to be that readers did also.

Lewis had discovered his own favorite allegorist, Edmund Spenser, early in 1916. His appreciation of Spenser's *Faerie Queene* increased through the years; and after living with Spenser's work for almost forty years Lewis finally published an essay about Spenser in 1954. In that essay he remarked wryly that some published fantasies of his own had had foisted on them many admirable allegorical meanings that he never dreamed of, some from the kindest critics. This experience made him doubt whether it is possible for the wit of man to devise anything in which the wit of some other man cannot find, with some justification, an unintended allegory.[5]

In this essay Lewis advises us that we shall understand actual allegory best by not trying too hard to understand it. Like loving, going to sleep, or behaving naturally, reading an allegory is done worst when we try hardest. We should surrender ourselves with childlike attention to the mood of the story. The worst thing we can do is to approach an allegory as if it were a complex puzzle to be solved. Lewis said this of *Faerie Queene*, but of course the same principle applies to *Pilgrim's Regress*.

Lewis also notes that a poet inventing with such energy as Spenser produces things that mean more than he knew or intended. For example, a place of imprisonment in the allegory may become, to some readers, a symbol of various kinds

---

5. C. S. Lewis, "Edmund Spenser, 1552–99," in *Major British Writers, Vol. 1*, ed. G. B. Harrison (New York: Harcourt, Brace & Co., 1954), 91–103. Collected in Lewis's *Studies in Medieval and Renaissance Literature* (Cambridge: Cambridge University Press, 1966).

of psychic imprisonment. This kind of literature, Lewis says, has psychotherapeutic powers if it is receptively read. Lewis did not claim so much for his own writing, allegorical or fantastic, but some readers have attributed that healing power to his fiction.

Lewis believed that the picture-language of allegory is ultimately derived from the unconscious; that it appeals to that level of our mind closest to the collective unconscious itself, the common pool of memory and responses that we all share as a race. But writers of allegory also use certain symbols which they expect their readers to consciously know and understand. If the reader of Spenser does not know the Bible and the classics, for example, many symbols are lost on him. That is also true for any reader of *Pilgrim's Regress*.

A couple of years after the publication of his essay on Spenser, Lewis contrasted allegory and myth in a personal letter to Father Peter Milward in 1956. Lewis said that in his view a good myth is a higher thing than an allegory. A writer puts into an allegory only what he already knows; he puts into a myth what he does not yet know and could not learn in any other way. Furthermore, an allegory has only one meaning, but a myth can yield ever varying meanings for different readers in different ages.[6]

Obviously, Lewis felt that Spenser's allegory—and, as he states hopefully in the preface to *Pilgrim's Regress,* possibly his own allegory—included bits of myth. Allegory's picture-language derives ultimately from the subconscious, but it is produced and understood by conscious use of fitting sym-

---

6. Lewis to Milward, 22 September 1956, *Letters of C. S. Lewis,* edited and with a memoir by W. H. Lewis, revised and enlarged edition edited by Walter Hooper (San Diego: Harcourt, Brace & Co., Harvest, 1993), 458.

bols. The author knows, allegory aside, what the points are, and tries to express them symbolically. In contrast, myth-making is a process of gradual discovery.

A reader once mistook the *Chronicles of Narnia* and *Perelandra* for allegories in a letter to Lewis. Lewis patiently tried to distinguish between allegory and "supposal" for her. He told her that allegory is a pictorial or literary composition in which immaterial realities are represented by fictitious physical objects. Thus Cupid allegorically represents the experience of erotic love and in *Pilgrim's Progress* a giant represents despair. Aslan of the *Chronicles of Narnia* does not represent the immaterial Deity as Giant Despair represents despair. Aslan is a supposal answering the question, "What might Christ become like if there really were a world like Narnia and He chose to be incarnate and die and rise again actually in *that* world as He has done in ours?" Granted the question, Christ would really have been a physical object in Narnia, as He was in our world.[7]

In contrast, it is a fact, not a supposal, that despair can capture and imprison a human soul. The fictitious part of Bunyan's allegory is the physical existence of the giant, the castle, and the dungeon.

Lewis would no doubt agree that the lizard on the young man's shoulder in his book *The Great Divorce* is an allegorical figure representing real lust as Cupid represents real erotic love. But the angels, the Bright Spirits, the dim souls, the journeying, the beauty, the dread, the solidity, the choices—all of these are fantasy. In the preface of *The Great Divorce* Lewis said, "I beg readers to remember that this is a fantasy. It has of course—or I intended it to have—a moral. But the

---

7. Lewis to Mrs. Hook, 29 December 1958, *Letters of C. S. Lewis*, 475.

transmortal conditions are solely an imaginative supposal."[8] No matter how much truth this supposal about the afterlife embodies, it is not allegory.

Lewis remarked once that he would be delighted if he found in heaven that Spenser had written six more books of *The Faerie Queene* there. Spenser had died before finishing it. Lewis, in turn, died before finishing a book he planned to write about Spenser. After Lewis's death, another Spenser scholar, Dr. Alastair Fowler, constructed the book from Lewis's terse, sometimes enigmatic, handwritten notes. It is titled *Spenser's Images of Life*.

In this brief book we find two more bits of advice that can guide us in reading *Pilgrim's Regress* or other allegories. First, there is the disparity to remember between what the allegorical people really count for in the universe and their own ideas of their adventures. We know that the characters are in an allegory, because we transcend the allegory. They cannot know it. There is an irony to their creaturely ignorance.[9]

Second, Lewis warns us through Fowler never to try to dispense with the allegorical figures by translating them into the realities they embody. For example, in *Pilgrim's Regress* John is rescued at one point by a tall, sun-bright virgin named Reason who rides a great black stallion and wields a sword. To substitute human reason for this great lady while reading the story would be fatal. Human reason is like the virgin Reason and is manifested to us more clearly in her. (Dr. Fowler kindly read and approved this entire essay about allegory before publication.)

---

8. C. S. Lewis, preface to *The Great Divorce* (New York: Macmillan, 1946), viii.
9. C. S. Lewis, *Spenser's Images of Life*, ed. Dr. Alastair Fowler (Cambridge: Cambridge University Press, 1967).

One of Lewis's most complex teachings about allegory is an expansion of the reminder in *Spenser's Images of Life* that characters in an allegory don't know that they are in an allegory. In *The Allegory of Love* Lewis explains the symbolist view that we, too, are in a sense allegorical figures—physical objects that represent a higher reality. Since that concept is extremely different from regular allegory, we must be sure to call it symbolism or sacramentalism instead. Lewis's description of the scene at the end of *The Great Divorce* in which the immortal souls of men and women stand around the silver table of time and watch the men and women as they appear to themselves and each other in their mortal lives is a good example of this kind of symbolism or sacramentalism. The men and women who were like chess figures did not know that they were, in a sense, allegorical figures.

Lewis's final insights into allegory and his view of *Pilgrim's Progress* in particular appeared in 1962 in his essay "The Vision of John Bunyan." His first major point is that allegory is a valid form only so long as it is doing what could not be done at all, or done so well, in any other way. When Bunyan infrequently lapsed into sermonizing instead of telling his story, then the allegory was frustrated and the image of the Road disappeared. Allegory gives you one thing in terms of another, and it is imperative to avoid confusion between the vehicle and its freight.[10]

Furthermore, in Bunyan's allegory the greater enters the lesser. The high theme was incarnated on the level of an adventure story; and not a story of high romance, at that, but a story full of humble details artfully told in the vernacular.

---

10. C. S. Lewis, "The Vision of John Bunyan," *Selected Literary Essays,* ed. Walter Hooper (Cambridge: Cambridge University Press, 1969), 146.

Accordingly, Lewis insisted upon an idiomatic style when he wrote *Pilgrim's Regress*.

Here again Lewis warned against reverting from allegorical images to ordinary conceptions. That moves you back to where you would be without the book. The right way is to keep moving into the book, not out of it. (Concentrate on Reason the armed virgin, not reason the intellectual process.) The right way is to keep moving from concept to image, because that enriches the concept. "And that is what allegory is for."[11]

Finally, Lewis refers to the urgency, the harsh woodcut energy, the continual sense of momentousness in *Pilgrim's Progress* which depend upon the flames of hell always flickering in the background. The story is thus full of ecstasies and terrors of immeasurable importance. Lewis admitted that many do not believe that either Bunyan's trumpets "with melodious noise" or the inferno await us where the road ends. But most people have discovered, Lewis supposed, "that to be born is to be exposed to delights and miseries greater than imagination could have anticipated; that the choice of ways at any cross-road may be more important than we think; and that short cuts may lead to very nasty places."[12]

Lewis first spoke those words on the BBC Radio thirty years after he wrote *Pilgrim's Regress*.[13] This is apparently the last recording of Lewis's voice, and it is apparently his last word on *Pilgrim's Progress*. It might now be taken as his last word on *Pilgrim's Regress* as well.

11. Ibid., 149.
12. Ibid., 153.
13. Lewis's 1962 radio lecture titled "The Pilgrim's Progress" is available on a cassette tape called *Comments and Critiques*, which may be purchased from the Episcopal Radio-TV Foundation, 3379 Peachtree Rd. NW, Suite 230, Atlanta, GA 30326; phone (404) 233-5419.

APPENDIX TWO

# REASON AND IMAGINATION: TWO HEMISPHERES OF KNOWING

A year after C. S. Lewis died on November 22, 1963, an especially important poem of his was published for the first time. It is sixteen lines long and appeared in 1964 in the collection titled *Poems*. Unfortunately, an editor gave this poem the title "Reason."[1] It should have been titled "Reason and Imagination." This poem relates closely to two of Lewis's most haunting books, *The Pilgrim's Regress* and *Till We Have Faces*, and it can lead readers to reflect upon Greek mythology, epistemology, and brain physiology. It is about truth.

In this poem the virgin goddess in armor, Athene, personifies reason. Lewis mentions the Acropolis, the highest point in Athens, where her colossal statue stood. (The entire city of

---

Early versions of this essay appeared in the *Journal of Psychology and Theology* (fall 1975) and *Mythlore* (winter 1979).
1. C. S. Lewis, *Poems*, ed. Walter Hooper (San Diego: Harcourt Brace Jovanovich, Harvest, 1977), 81.

Athens was named for its protector Athene.) Readers of *Pilgrim's Regress* recognize Athene in the armed virgin named Reason. Readers of *Till We Have Faces* recognize the wisdom of Athene in the figure of the Fox.

Following are the lines and fragments of lines that refer to reason in this poem:

> Set on the soul's acropolis the reason stands
> A virgin, arm'd, commercing with celestial light,
> And he who sins against her has defiled his own
> Virginity: no cleansing makes his garment white;
> So clear is reason. . . .
> Tempt not Athene. . . .
> . . . maid . . .
> . . . height
> . . . intellectual sight

In contrast, in this poem the mother goddess Demeter personifies imagination. In Greek mythology Demeter stood for harvest and fertility. No Greek city was named after her, but the Eleusinian Mysteries were inaugurated in her honor. According to myth, Demeter wandered to Eleusis while grieving for her daughter Persephone, who had been abducted to the underworld by Pluto. Processions of Athenians used to travel the twelve miles from Athens to Eleusis for an annual fall festival. Little is known about the secret Eleusinian Mysteries. Demeter is far more mysterious than Athene.

Following are the lines and fragments of lines that refer to imagination in Lewis's poem:

> . . . But how dark imagining,
> Warm, dark, obscure and infinite, daughter of Night:
> Dark is her brow, the beauty of her eyes with sleep

Is loaded, and her pains are long, and her delight.
. . . Wound not in her fertile pains
Demeter, nor rebel against her mother-right.
. . . mother
. . . depth . . .
. . . imagination's dim exploring touch

In the last six lines of this undated poem Lewis wishes that Athene and Demeter would agree with each other in his own mind. He wishes that his two modes of knowing, reason and imagination, would together teach him the truth. Only then could Lewis wholly say that he believed. Neither mental function is complete without the other.

I am not aware of a live figure typifying imagination in Lewis's fiction. But I am reminded of Orual's question in *Till We Have Faces:* "Why must holy places be dark places?" and the confession of her teacher, the Fox, "I never told her why the old Priest got something from the dark House that I never got from my trim sentences. . . . Of course, I didn't know. . . . I don't know now."[2]

In *Till We Have Faces* Christlike Psyche chose to descend to the underworld of Demeter's daughter Persephone to get beauty from death to bring back up for others. And in *Pilgrim's Regress* John had to descend into catacombs under the earth where he learned many mysteries and died many deaths. It was down there that the voice of God said to him about mythology, "It is but truth, not fact: an image, not the very real. . . . [T]his is the veil under which I have chosen to appear even from the first until now. For this end I made your senses and for this end your imagination, that you might see

2. C. S. Lewis, *Till We Have Faces* (New York: Harcourt, Brace & Co., 1957), 249, 295.

My face and live. . . . [W]as there any age in any land when men did not know that corn and wine were the blood and body of a dying and yet living God?"[3]

In *A Circle of Quiet* Madeleine L'Engle stated, "It is . . . through the world of the imagination which takes us beyond the restrictions of provable fact, that we touch the hem of truth."[4]

In Paul Tournier's *Naming of Persons* he talked about that same "dim exploring touch." Tournier remarked that Saint Paul knew that the most convincing revelations could not be expressed in rational discourse. The revelation which overtook him on the Damascus Road was not didactic teaching or intellectual proposition. After all his theological argument in 2 Corinthians, Paul finally turned to that Damascus Road mystical experience to establish his ultimate spiritual authority. And Paul points out that he felt the thing as an almost physical experience: "[W]hether in the body or out of the body I do not know; God knows" (2 Corinthians 12:2 NRSV). What happened to Paul was not on the level of lucid thought, but on the mysterious level of the incarnate person. "Is it not of that same level that we are speaking," Tournier presses on, "profound, obscure and organic—when we refer to the recording of the mother's voice on the mind of the child she is carrying in her womb?"[5]

Reason usually resides in the left hemisphere of the brain. That is where words and mathematics usually work; that is the physical seat of sequential logic. That is where we grasp the continuity of history and where the Fox's "trim sen-

---

3. *The Pilgrim's Regress,* deluxe illustrated edition (Grand Rapids, Mich.: William B. Eerdmans Publishing, 1981), book 9, chap. 5, p. 169.
4. Madeleine L'Engle, *A Circle of Quiet* (Greenwich, Conn.: Fawcett, 1975), 112.
5. Paul Tournier, *The Naming of Persons* (New York: Harper & Row, 1974), 96.

tences" were created. That is where Lewis wrote *Mere Christianity* and *Oxford History of English Literature in the Sixteenth Century.*

In the human body, the corpus callosum is an inconceivably complex bundle of nerves coordinating the two halves of the brain. Imagination, so far as it is concerned with images, lives in the right hemisphere of the brain, which is spatial and mute. Damage to the left hemisphere can destroy a person's ability to use words, and damage to the right hemisphere can destroy a person's ability to recognize faces. Lewis couldn't have consciously known that when he wrote *Till We Have Faces*, but it fits exactly. In *Pilgrim's Regress*, God told John in the depths of the catacombs, "[F]or this end [I made] your imagination, that you might see My face."[6]

The right hemisphere is where dreaming takes place (*Pilgrim's Regress* is told as a dream), and the left is where we analyze our dreams. The right seems to be the source of creative intuition. Lewis claimed that his fiction all began with images that sprang into his consciousness unbidden, such as the image of a faun in snowy woods that gave rise to the *Chronicles of Narnia*.

It might seem a long way from children's fantasy to contemporary physics and subnuclear particles. In 1964 Hideki Yukawa, winner of the Nobel Prize in physics, gave an address in Athens, the city of reason. Yukawa said that abstract thought needs to be balanced by intuition, with which Greek and Chinese geniuses in ancient times were richly endowed. Yukawa used the Japanese word *kan,* which means a kind of sensibility or alertness that we call intuition

---

6. *Pilgrim's Regress,* book 9, chap. 5, p. 169.

in English.[7] (C. S. Lewis and Hideki Yukawa shared an unusual characteristic in addition to creativity and mental dexterity; both men suffered from a frustrating lack of manual dexterity. Both had unusually clumsy hands.)

Robert Ornstein claims in *Psychology of Consciousness*, "The polarity and the integration of these two modes of consciousness, the complementary workings of the intellect and the intuition, underlie our highest achievements."[8]

In his 1939 essay "Bluspels and Flalansferes" Lewis wrote, "I am a rationalist. For me, reason is the natural organ of truth; but imagination is the organ of meaning."[9] He continued, "If there is not, in fact, a kind of psycho-physical parallelism (or more) in the universe—then all our thinking is nonsensical. But we cannot, without contradiction, believe it to be nonsensical. And so, admittedly, the view I have taken has metaphysical implications. But so has every view."

Does brain physiology show that reason is nothing but left hemisphere cortical activity and imagination is nothing but right hemisphere cortical activity? Lewis warned about this use of "nothing but" in his essay "Transposition." "[I]t seems to me very likely that the real relation between mind and body is one of Transposition. We are certain that, in this life at any rate, thought is intimately connected with the brain. The theory that thought therefore is merely a movement in the brain is, in my opinion, nonsense."[10]

---

7. Hideki Yukawa, "Intuition and Abstraction in Scientific Thinking," in *Creativity and Intuition: A Physicist Looks at East and West* (New York: Kodansha International, 1973), 100–109.
8. Robert E. Ornstein, *The Psychology of Consciousness* (New York: Harcourt Brace Jovanovich, 1977), 36.
9. C. S. Lewis, "Bluspels and Flalansferes: A Semantic Nightmare," in *Rehabilitations* (London: Oxford University Press, 1939), 157. Also collected in *Selected Literary Essays* (Cambridge: Cambridge University Press, 1969), 265.
10. C. S. Lewis, "Transposition," in *Transposition and Other Addresses* (London:

But he was aware of the powerful influence of the reductionism that he denounced in *Pilgrim's Regress* as the Spirit of the Age. "[P]hysiology never can find anything in thought except twitchings of the grey matter. . . .

. . . "There will always be evidence, and every month fresh evidence, to show that religion is only psychological, justice only self-protection, politics only economics, love only lust, and thought itself only cerebral biochemistry."[11]

In recent years there has been a slight shift away from this reductionistic behaviorism that Lewis detested. I think he would have appreciated a claim made by Roger Sperry, professor of psychobiology at Cal Tech:

> After more than 50 years of strict behaviorist avoidance of such terms as "mental imagery" and visual, verbal, auditory "images," in the past five years these terms have come into wide usage as explanatory constructs in the literature on cognition, perception, and other higher functions.
>
> The revised interpretation brings the conscious mind into the causal sequence in human decision making—and therefore into behavior generally—and thus back into the realm of experimental science from which it has long been excluded. This swing in psychology and neuroscience away from hardcore materialism and reductionism toward a new, more acceptable brand of mentalism tends now to restore to the scientific image of human nature some of the dignity, freedom, and other humanistic attributes of which it had been deprived by the behavioristic approach.[12]

Geoffrey Bles, 1949), 16. Revised and expanded edition, ed. Walter Hooper (New York: Macmillan, 1980), 63.
11. Lewis, "Transposition," 1980 ed., 64, 72.
12. Roger W. Sperry, "Left-brain, Right-brain," *Saturday Review*, 9 August 1975, 32.

In *Pilgrim's Regress*, Lewis's first prose fiction, he clearly says "Tempt not Athene." Reason is a great heroine. But in *Till We Have Faces*, his last prose fiction, he clearly says "Wound not in her fertile pains / Demeter." The main character, Orual, is outraged that deity draws near at times in dreams and visions but refuses to answer our clear questions. At the end of her life she finally understands: "I know now, Lord, why you utter no answer. You are yourself the answer. Before your face questions die away. What other answer would suffice? Only words, words; to be led out to battle against other words . . ."[13]

Orual desired that her autobiography *(Till We Have Faces)* should be read in ancient Greece. Her creator, C. S. Lewis, obviously desired that both *Pilgrim's Regress* and *Till We Have Faces* should be read in our own culture. And he wanted his poem about reason and imagination to be read also.

Paraphrased, this poem concludes with a question he asks for himself and his readers: Oh, who will reconcile in me the high, virginal, clear-sighted intellect with the deep, dim, motherly imagination? With those two agreeing about truth, then I could truly and *wholly* say that I believe!

More than anyone else, for many readers, the answer is C. S. Lewis himself.

# APPENDIX THREE

# THE YEARS OF THE LIFE OF C. S. LEWIS

**Nine Years of Irish Childhood**
1898 Born at Belfast, November 28
1899 Infancy
1900 "Talking like anything" (his mother said)
1901 Told riddles with brother Warren
1902 Chose the name Jacksie for life
1903 Began learning chess
1904 Unusual rain kept boys indoors more than usual
1905 Family moved to "Little Lea" in County Down
1906 First trip to London; enjoyed mice at the zoo most
1907 Vacation at beach in France; began diary

**Twenty-Three Years of Serious Academic Pursuits**
1908 Mother died; boys sent to England for schooling
1909 Suffered at terrible boarding school
1910 Entered Campbell school in Belfast; dropped out ill

1911  Entered Cherbourg school; lost childhood faith
1912  Discovered Wagner and "Northernness"
1913  Won scholarship to Malvern College
1914  Met Arthur Greeves and W. T. Kirkpatrick
1915  Discovered writings of George MacDonald
1916  Was accepted at Oxford
1917  Entered the army and the Moore family
1918  Was wounded in France; returned to England
1919  Published *Spirits in Bondage* (early poems)
1920  Academic success in philosophy
1921  Visited William Butler Yeats
1922  Academic success in the classics
1923  Academic success in English literature
1924  First employment, at University College, Oxford
1925  Permanent position at Magdalen College, Oxford
1926  Published book-length poem *Dymer*
1927  Began first novel ("The Most Substantial People")
1928  Began writing *The Allegory of Love*
1929  Regained belief in God; father died
1930  Moved into permanent home, the Kilns

**Twenty-Three Christian Years of Accomplishments**
1931  Accepted Christianity
1932  Wrote *The Pilgrim's Regress*
1933  Published *The Pilgrim's Regress*
1934  Visited Scotland and Ireland with Warren
1935  Completed *The Allegory of Love* for publication
1936  Discovered writings of Charles Williams
1937  Wrote *The Personal Heresy* with Tillyard
1938  Published *Out of the Silent Planet*
1939  End of his annual walking tours
1940  Published *The Problem of Pain*
1941  Began series of twenty-five wartime radio broadcasts

1942 Published *The Screwtape Letters*
1943 Published *The Abolition of Man* and *Perelandra*
1944 Published *Beyond Personality*
1945 Published *The Great Divorce, That Hideous Strength*
1946 Honorary Doctor of Divinity, St. Andrews University
1947 Published *Miracles*
1948 Published *Arthurian Torso*
1949 Published two collections of essays
1950 Published first of *The Chronicles of Narnia*
1951 "Foster mother," Mrs. Moore, died
1952 Honorary Doctor of Literature, Laval University
1953 Friendship with Joy Davidman grew

**Nine Years of Greatest Joys and Losses**
1954 Promoted to post at Cambridge University
1955 Published autobiography *Surprised by Joy*
1956 Published *Till We Have Faces,* his favorite
1957 Married Joy Davidman, in her hospital room
1958 Published *Reflections on the Psalms*
1959 Wife Joy suffered cancer relapse
1960 Published *The Four Loves;* his wife died
1961 Published *A Grief Observed,* about his bereavement
1962 Began *Letters to Malcolm,* on prayer
1963 Died on November 22, just before sixty-fifth birthday

# SELECT BIBLIOGRAPHY

## *A Reader's Guide for Study of* The Pilgrim's Regress

### Compiled by Kathryn Lindskoog and David Mortimer

Unless otherwise noted, citations in this bibliography refer to the American editions and to revised or updated editions. *Regress (The Pilgrim's Regress)* refers to the Eerdmans 1981 edition.

I.   EARLY REVIEWS OF *PILGRIM'S REGRESS*
II.  WRITINGS BY C. S. LEWIS MENTIONED IN *FINDING THE LANDLORD*
III. MEDIEVAL DREAM VISION LITERATURE AND CRITICAL EVALUATIONS OF *PILGRIM'S REGRESS*

### EARLY REVIEWS OF *PILGRIM'S REGRESS*

*America* 54 (4 January 1936): 305. Reviewer Steward E. Dollard mistakes Mother Kirk for the Catholic Church: "The author traces the story of a modern Pilgrim's journey from the land of strict Calvinism to the Roman Catholic Faith." Mentions Lewis's telling but not bitter satire.

*Blackfriars* 17 (4 January 1936): 69–70. Reviewer G. S. Sayer refers to the book's "remarkable acuity" and concludes, "[T]he revival of the allegorical method is very successful; thereby Mr. Lewis can treat of profound and complex things in a simple way."

*Catholic World: A Monthly Magazine of General Literature and Science* 143 (May 1936): 239–40. Reviewer Bertrand L. Conway writes that *Regress* is "brilliantly written" and "a caustic, devastating critique of modern philosophy, religion, politics and art."

*Downside Review* 54 (January 1936): 138–39. Reviewer finds humor, mastery of dialogue, and satiric irony in *Regress* and calls it "[a] notable contribution to Catholic literature."

*Living Church* 94 (11 January 1936): 46. Reviewer W. Norman Pittenger assumes *Regress* is a Roman Catholic work after Bunyan's classic: "We are sure the book will find many delighted readers, even if they do not all arrive in the happy haven of Roman Catholicism." He praises its "delightful lightness and wit."

*New York Times Book Review,* 8 December 1935, 7. Reviewer Jane Spence Southron rates *Regress* highly on its literary merits and allegorical characters: "On its literary side the book deserves high rating. The allegorical characters are not just abstractions. They are . . . objectively real and subjectively true to their inner meaning."

*Presbyterian Guardian,* 22 June 1936, 117, 141. Reviewer Henry G. Welbon mistakes Lewis for a Roman Catholic, disagrees with his theology, and inexplicably notes, "[L]ittle of his own theology can be traced in the book."

*Times Literary Supplement* (London), 6 July 1933, 456. The reviewer admires Lewis's narrative and poetry: "When John . . . begins to find the way to Salvation he is inspired to break into fragments of song . . . revealing a poetic gift that may rightly be called arresting: it pulls the reader up in the midst of the smooth-flowing narrative to admire its energy and profundity."

## Writings by C. S. Lewis Mentioned in *Finding the Landlord*

[Clive Hamilton, pseud.]. *Spirits in Bondage: A Cycle of Lyrics.* London: William Heinemann, 1919. Reprint, edited by Walter Hooper, San Diego: Harcourt Brace Jovanovich, Harvest, 1984. This book is now included in *The Collected Poems of C. S. Lewis,* ed. Walter Hooper (London: HarperCollins, 1994), 157–224. Lewis considers nature wholly diabolical and malevolent; God, if He exists, is outside and in opposition to the cosmic arrangement. The poem titled "Our Daily Bread" foreshadows *Regress.* In the last three stanzas Lewis claims that often in ordinary places he suddenly hears the call of Living voices, catches sight of lands beyond the wall, and sees a strange god's face. Someday, he predicts, this experience will force him to leave home and become a pilgrim, wandering in foreign places. In "Song of the Pilgrims," seekers for a beautiful garden of eternal life lament the travail of their unsuccessful search, but doggedly reaffirm their goal. "Death in Battle" expresses the hope of a dying man for an island in the West that is the garden of God.

[Clive Hamilton, pseud.]. *Dymer.* London: J. M. Dent; New York: E. P. Dutton, 1926. Reprint, with a new preface by C. S. Lewis, London: J. M. Dent; New York: Macmillan, 1950. Reprinted in *Narrative Poems,* ed. Walter Hooper (London: Geoffrey Bles, 1969; New York: Harcourt Brace Jovanovich, 1972; Harcourt Brace Jovanovich, Harvest, 1979), 3–91. In this book-length poem begun in 1922 Lewis traces the strange adventures of a young man who was born in the "Perfect City" but rebelled and left. This is in a sense the opposite of Bunyan's *Pilgrim's Progress,* in which the pilgrim was born in the City of Destruction but rebelled and left. Dymer represents a man escaping from illusion, particularly the illusion of Joy. At the end of the story he is killed by a monster. In his preface to the 1950 edition, Lewis explains some aspects of this rather bitter allegory and describes the mythlike basis of the book.

*The Pilgrim's Regress: An Allegorical Apology for Christianity, Reason and Romanticism.* London: J. M. Dent, 1933; New York: Sheed & Ward, 1935. Reprint, with Lewis's preface, six footnotes, and running headlines, London: Geoffrey Bles, 1943; New York: Sheed & Ward, 1944; Grand Rapids, Mich.: William B. Eerdmans Publishing, 1958. Notes by

John C. Traupman (printed with new plates; included Lewis's preface but not his running headlines), New York: Bantam, 1981. Illustrated by Michael Hague with Lewis's 1943 preface (presented as an afterword) and running headlines, Grand Rapids, Mich.: William B. Eerdmans Publishing, 1981. Lewis dedicated the book to his lifelong friend, Arthur Greeves.

*The Allegory of Love: A Study in Medieval Tradition.* London and New York: Oxford University Press, 1936. Reprint, with corrections, London: Oxford University Press, 1938; New York: Oxford University Press, Galaxy, 1958. Lewis worked on this study of the allegorical love poetry of the Middle Ages for eight years and wrote his own prose allegory, *Pilgrim's Regress,* during that period. Lewis explains that an allegorist starts with an immaterial fact such as wrath and then invents a fictitious material object such as a person to depict wrath. Lewis differentiates allegory from symbolism or sacramentalism, in which we humans are in a sense allegorical figures—physical objects that represent a higher reality.

"Bluspels and Flalansferes: A Semantic Nightmare." In *Rehabilitations and Other Essays.* London: Oxford University Press, 1939. Also reprinted in *Selected Literary Essays,* ed. Walter Hooper (Cambridge: Cambridge University Press, 1969), 251–65. In this essay Lewis examines the limits and strengths of metaphor and contends that with imagination new metaphors may be invented and old ones may be brought back to life. "For all of us there are things which we cannot fully understand at all, but of which we can get a faint inkling by means of metaphor" (p. 254). Plato was "among the great creators of metaphor, and therefore among the masters of meaning" (p. 265). Lewis also cites Bunyan and Dante as greats. As reason is the organ of truth, imagination is the organ of meaning. Book 8, chapters 3–5 of *Regress* include John's discovery of his use of metaphors for the Landlord. The Man (Christ) said to John: "Your life has been saved all this day by crying out to something which you call by many names, and you have said to yourself that you used metaphors" (p. 140).

"Christianity and Culture." *Theology* 40 (March 1940): 166–79. Reprinted under same title (with two letters from Lewis) in *Christian Reflections,* ed. Walter Hooper (London: Geoffrey Bles; Grand Rapids, Mich.: William B. Eerdmans Publishing, 1967), 12–36. This essay describes religious dangers that beset cultured people and religious dangers that beset uncultured people. Both are exemplified in *Regress.*

*A Preface to "Paradise Lost": Being the Ballard Matthews Lectures Delivered at University College, North Wales, 1941, Revised and Enlarged.* London: Oxford University Press, 1942; New York: Oxford University Press, Galaxy, 1961. In this book dedicated to Charles Williams, Lewis contrasts correct and incorrect interpretations of Milton's epic, and examines Milton's theology. Near the end of his study (p. 137), Lewis criticizes T. S. Eliot's anti-Romantic approach to literature. Lewis's Mr. Angular in *Regress* is a satirical complaint about T. S. Eliot.

"Dogma and the Universe." Parts 1 and 2. Part 2 titled "Dogma and Science." *Guardian,* 19 March 1943, 96; 26 March 1943, 104, 107. Reprinted in *God in the Dock: Essays on Theology and Ethics,* ed. Walter Hooper (Grand Rapids, Mich.: William B. Eerdmans Publishing, 1970), 38–47 and *Undeceptions: Essays on Theology and Ethics,* ed. Walter Hooper (London: Geoffrey Bles, 1971). In this essay Lewis defends Christianity and attacks scientism, the dogma taught by Mr. Enlightenment in *Regress.* John's experience in book 10 of *Regress* seems to foreshadow the following statement in this essay: "When any man comes into the presence of God he will find, whether he wishes it or not, that all those things which seemed to make him so different from the men of other times, or even from his earlier self, have fallen off him. He is back where he always was, where every man always is. *Eadem sunt omnia semper.* ['Everything is always the same']" (p. 47).

"'Bulverism,'" *Socratic Digest,* no. 2 (June 1944): 16–20. Reprinted in *God in the Dock: Essays on Theology and Ethics,* ed. Walter Hooper (Grand Rapids, Mich.: William B. Eerdmans Publishing, 1970), 271–77 and *Undeceptions: Essays on Theology and Ethics,* ed. Walter Hooper (London: Geoffrey Bles, 1971). Lewis invents the word "Bulverism" to expose the dishonesty of combating a statement by ignoring its merits and attacking the purported mind-set of the person who made it. Lewis insists, "[Y]ou must show *that* a man is wrong before you start explaining *why* he is wrong" (p. 273). In book 3, chapter 8 of *Regress,* the jailor taught his prisoners that if you explain *why* a person is wrong you never have to show *that* the person is wrong. In the prisoners' catechism, argument is "the attempted rationalization of the arguer's desires" (p. 49).

"Religion and Science," *Coventry Evening Telegraph,* 3 January 1945, 4. Reprinted in *God in the Dock: Essays on Theology and Ethics,* ed. Walter Hooper (Grand Rapids, Mich.: William B. Eerdmans Publishing, 1970), 72–75 and *Undeceptions: Essays on Theology and Ethics,* ed. Walter Hooper (London: Geoffrey Bles, 1971). In the form of this short dialogue between friends, Lewis debunks the kind of attitude that Mr. Enlightenment represented in *Regress.* Lewis argues that reality is much more complex and includes far more distant horizons than popularized science is willing to admit.

*The Great Divorce: A Dream.* London: Geoffrey Bles, Centenary Press, 1945; New York: Macmillan, 1946; Macmillan, 1963. In this fantasy that Lewis liked much better than *Screwtape Letters,* he describes a busload of residents of hell who took an outing to the outskirts of heaven. Although they were urged to stay, most of them preferred to return to hell. In book 2, chapter 3 of *Regress,* Virtue's slogan was that to travel hopefully is better than to arrive (a quotation from Robert Louis Stevenson); in *The Great Divorce* the Apostate Bishop makes the same claim. In book 7, chapter 12 of *Regress,* Wisdom spoke of the difference between the wishes of our mortal selves and the wishes of our real and eternal selves; in the last chapter of *The Great Divorce* Lewis presents the difference in a dramatic way. There a great assembly of gigantic forms stand in deep silence around a small silver table (named Time). On the table are little figures like chessmen that represent people as they appear to one another in the world, and the great silent watchers are the immortal souls of those very people.

*George MacDonald: An Anthology.* Edited and with a preface by C. S. Lewis. London: Geoffrey Bles, 1946; New York: Macmillan, 1947; Macmillan, Collier, 1986. This collection contains 365 excerpts from the works of George MacDonald. Lewis selected some of his favorite short passages from MacDonald's sermons, fantasies, novels, and poetry. Number 279, which describes the step of faith in conversion, "You must throw yourself in," seems to foreshadow book 9, chapter 4 in *Regress* where John must throw himself in. Number 289, which describes a protagonist who dreams that he is awake, seems to foreshadow book 7, chapter 7 in *Regress* where the protagonist dreams he is awake.

*Miracles: A Preliminary Study.* London: Geoffrey Bles, Centenary Press; New York: Macmillan, 1947. In this analysis Lewis explains the nature of the miraculous: that God's truth first appears in mythical form, and later becomes incarnate as historical fact. Myth is "a real though unfocussed gleam of divine truth falling on human imagination." The mythology of the people of Israel is "chosen by God to be the vehicle of the earliest sacred truths, the first step in that process which ends in the New Testament where truth has become entirely historical" (p. 161). In book 9, chapter 5 of *Regress* Christ told John, "[I]t is My mythology. . . . [T]his is My inventing, this is the veil under which I have chosen to appear even from the first until now" (p. 169).

*Mere Christianity: A Revised and Amplified Edition, with a New Introduction, of the Three Books "Broadcast Talks," "Christian Behaviour," and "Beyond Personality."* London: Geoffrey Bles; New York: Macmillan, 1952; Macmillan, 1960. (The American editions changed the title of *Broadcast Talks* to *The Case for Christianity*.) A lucid apologetic for Christianity which defines the longing or *Sehnsucht* which John experienced with the Island in *Regress* and Lewis described in his spiritual autobiography *Surprised by Joy:* "If I find in myself a desire which no experience in this world can satisfy, the most probable explanation is that I was made for another world. . . . Probably earthly pleasures were never meant to satisfy it, but only to arouse it, to suggest the real thing. . . . I must keep alive in myself the desire for my true country, which I shall not find till after death" (p. 120).

"Edmund Spenser, 1552–99." In *Major British Writers,* edited by G. B. Harrison, 91–103. Vol. 1. New York: Harcourt, Brace & Co., 1954. Also reprinted in *Studies in Medieval and Renaissance Literature,* comp. Walter Hooper (Cambridge: Cambridge University Press, 1966). Lewis advises that allegory is best understood by not trying too hard to understand it. Like loving, going to sleep, or behaving naturally, reading an allegory is done worst when we try hardest. Allegory is not to be approached as if it were a complex puzzle to be solved. Lewis also notes that a poet inventing with such energy as Spenser produces things that mean more than he knew or intended. For example, a place of imprisonment in the allegory may become, to some readers, a symbol of various kinds of psychic imprisonment. This kind of literature, Lewis says, has psychotherapeutic powers if it is receptively read. The picture-language of allegory is ultimately derived from the unconscious, and it appeals to that level of our mind closest to the collective unconscious itself, the common pool of memory and responses that we all share as a race.

*Surprised by Joy: The Shape of My Early Life.* London: Geoffrey Bles, 1955; New York: Harcourt, Brace & World, 1956; New York: Harcourt Brace Jovanovich, 1956; Harcourt Brace Jovanovich, Harvest, 1966. In this spiritual autobiography Lewis recasts the story of *Regress,* including the role that *Sehnsucht* played in his conversion to Christianity. In both books, Lewis tells how he lived through a succession of attempts to attain what he calls Joy, and eventually arrived at his goal. Various images and sensations "if idolatrously mistaken for Joy itself, soon honestly confessed themselves inadequate" (p. 220). Lewis calls this pattern of sidetracking and correction the "dialectic of desire." For example, in chapter 5 of *Surprised by Joy* Lewis tells of his own futile search for Joy in Nordic mythology and literary expertise, and in book 2, chapter 5 of *Regress* he tells of John's temporary infatuation with Media Halfways. In chapter 13 of *Surprised by Joy,* he warns against Freudian reductionism; and in book 3, chapter 6 of *Regress* he warns against it allegorically. In *Surprised by Joy* the "dialectic of desire" finally led Lewis to God, and he realized that "total surrender, the absolute leap in the dark, were demanded" (p. 228). Similarly, in book 9, chapter 4 of *Regress,* John realized that he had to throw himself down head first into deep, dark waters.

*Till We Have Faces: A Myth Retold.* London: Geoffrey Bles, 1956; New York: Harcourt, Brace & Co., 1957; Grand Rapids, Mich.: William B. Eerdmans Paperback, 1966. This was Lewis's favorite of all his books. It was his last book of fiction, and it made extraordinary use of themes from his first book of fiction, *Regress.* An aged pagan queen named Orual has written an autobiographical complaint to the gods, and it forms the substance of the book's narrative. In her story the wisdom of her tutor, a slave from Greece, resembles that of the armed virgin named Reason in *Regress.* Like John in *Regress,* Orual fears the Mountain and wants nothing to do with the god of the Mountain, although her beloved sister Psyche longs for him. "Do you think it all meant nothing, all the longing? The longing for home? For indeed it now feels not like going, but like going back. All my life the god of the Mountain has been wooing me. Oh, look up once at least before the end and wish me joy. I am going to my lover" (p. 76). Psyche descends to the underworld to get beauty from death to bring back up for others, as in book 9, chapter 5 of *Regress* where John eventually descends into the catacombs under the earth to learn many mysteries and die many deaths.

"The Vision of John Bunyan," *Listener* 68 (13 December 1962): 1006–8. Reprinted in *Selected Literary Essays*, ed. Walter Hooper (Cambridge: Cambridge University Press, 1969), 146–53. Lewis's final comments on allegory appeared in this critique of *Pilgrim's Progress*. Here Lewis defends allegory as a valid form of literary expression "only so long as it is doing what could not be done at all, or done so well, in any other way" (p. 146). When Bunyan infrequently lapsed into sermonizing instead of telling his story, the allegory was frustrated and the image of the Road disappeared. Furthermore, in reading allegory "we ought not to be thinking 'This green valley where the shepherd boy is singing, represents humility'; we ought to be discovering, as we read, that humility is like that green valley" (p. 149). Bunyan's high theme was incarnated on the level of an adventure story; and not a story of high romance, at that, but a story full of humble details artfully told in the vernacular. Similarly, Lewis intentionally wrote *Regress* in an idiomatic style.

*The Discarded Image: An Introduction to Medieval and Renaissance Literature.* Cambridge: Cambridge University Press, 1964, 1967, 1970. Lewis provides historical background needed for full understanding of Medieval and Renaissance literature. He points out that the culture of the Middle Ages was extremely bookish and fond of systematizing. On pages 60–69 Lewis summarizes the teachings of the Latin philosopher Macrobius (circa A.D. 400), author of *Cicero's Dream of Scipio*. Macrobius transmitted the incomparable dream interpretation system of Artemidorius (circa A.D. 100). The first of five types of dreams in this system is *somnium,* which "shows us truths veiled in an allegorical form" (p. 63). It is obvious that *Regress* is in the medieval tradition of the "feignedsomnia," and that Lewis knew it, although the immediate model for his dream allegory was *Pilgrim's Progress.*

*Poems.* Edited by Walter Hooper. London: Geoffrey Bles, 1964; Harcourt, Brace & World, 1965; New York: Harcourt Brace Jovanovich, Harvest, 1977. *Poems* is reprinted, along with *Spirits in Bondage* and "A Miscellany of Additional Poems" in *The Collected Poems of C. S. Lewis,* ed. Walter Hooper (London: HarperCollins, 1994). Of the 122 poems in *Poems,* 75 were published in Lewis's lifetime; of those, 45 are revised and 13 have been retitled. Because the original versions are often much better than the unexplained 1964 revisions, they are preferable. For example, "The Day with a White Mark" is apt to delight readers of *Regress,* but Lewis's version in *Punch* (217 [17 August 1949]: 170), is superior to the version in *Poems.*

*Letters of C. S. Lewis.* Edited and with a memoir by W. H. Lewis. London: Geoffrey Bles, 1966; New York: Harcourt, Brace & World, 1966; Harcourt Brace Jovanovich, Harvest, 1975. Rev. and enl. Edited by Walter Hooper. London: Collins, Fount, 1988; San Diego: Harcourt, Brace & Co., Harvest, 1993. This collection of letters by Lewis's brother, Warren Lewis, was initially intended to be used as a biographical account. (Some of the alleged history and derogatory material about Warren Lewis in the introduction to the revised 1988 edition is not universally accepted by Lewis scholars.) C. S. Lewis's collected letters are invaluable in several ways. In often scintillating, quotable prose they provide candid glimpses of his personal life, his literary pursuits, his spiritual growth, his pastoral role, his intellectual perspicacity, his affections, enthusiasms, opinions, and wit.

"The Funeral of a Great Myth." In *Christian Reflections,* edited by Walter Hooper, 82–93. London: Geoffrey Bles; Grand Rapids, Mich.: William B. Eerdmans Publishing, 1967. This essay is Lewis's attack upon popular evolutionism (not evolution as a biological theorem). Lewis satirized assumptions like this with the words of Mr. Enlightenment in *Regress.*

*Spenser's Images of Life.* Edited by Dr. Alastair Fowler. Cambridge: Cambridge University Press, 1967. Fowler constructed this Lewis book from Lewis's terse, sometimes enigmatic, handwritten notes. Lewis taught that there is a disparity between what the allegorical people really count for in the universe and their own ideas of their adventures. (We know that the characters are in an allegory because we transcend the allegory. They cannot know it. There is an irony to their creaturely ignorance.) Readers of allegory must never dispense with allegorical figures by translating them into the realities they embody.

*They Stand Together: The Letters of C. S. Lewis to Arthur Greeves (1914–1963).* Edited by Walter Hooper. London: Collins, 1979; New York: Macmillan, 1979. Lewis's letters to his friend Arthur Greeves spanned forty-nine years. They provide insight into many of Lewis's thoughts, feelings, and experiences, some of which are related to *Regress*. For example, in the letter dated 13 April 1930 Lewis registered his mixed response to Virginia Woolf's *Orlando* (1928), including his complaint: "the usual stale cynicism . . . in fact all the tricks of the clevers" (p. 348). This corresponds to book 3 of *Regress*.

*All My Road Before Me: The Diary of C. S. Lewis 1922–1927.* Edited by Walter Hooper. London: HarperCollins, 1991; San Diego: Harcourt Brace Jovanovich, Harvest, 1991. This diary of the young preconversion Lewis chronicles domestic trivia, literary endeavors, readings in classics and philosophy, and aspirations and frustrations in applying for employment. Vivid entries from February through April 1923 record the nightmarish terrors of a slowly dying friend who moved into Lewis's home. This experience, which inspired Lewis's unfinished, unpublished 1927 novel, "The Most Substantial People," may have contributed also to the description of John's Uncle George in book 1, chapter 3 of *Regress*. Lewis's headline in this chapter describes an uncomfortable funeral "lacking both Pagan fortitude and Christian hope" (p. 10). Lewis also records a satirical literary hoax intended to trick T. S. Eliot (pp. 410–14); Mr. Angular is a caricature of Eliot in *Regress*.

*The Collected Poems of C. S. Lewis.* Edited by Walter Hooper. London: HarperCollins, 1994. Includes *Spirits in Bondage, Poems,* and "A Miscellany of Additional Poems." The new "Introductory Letter of 1963 by C. S. Lewis" at the front of this book seems boorish and has questionable provenance. The last section includes Lewis's poignant sixteen-line poem "Your True Antiquities," which relates to book 10, chapter 10 of *Regress*. Unfortunately, "Your True Antiquities" is hidden in the middle of a vastly inferior, unLewisian poem called "Finchley Avenue" on pages 250–52.

## Medieval Dream Vision Literature and Critical Evaluations of *Pilgrim's Regress*

Aeschliman, Michael D. *The Restitution of Man: C. S. Lewis and the Case Against Scientism*. Grand Rapids, Mich.: William B. Eerdmans Publishing, 1983. In this short but detailed work, Aeschliman examines Lewis's case against scientism. Although *Regress* is largely passed over (he concentrates on Lewis's nonfiction such as *The Abolition of Man*, 1943), this book skillfully summarizes Lewis's attack on the dogma taught by Mr. Enlightenment in *Regress*. Placing Lewis's apologetics in the perspective of history, Aeschliman writes, "As Dr. Johnson fought the impiously excessive rationalism of the eighteenth century, Chesterton and Lewis fought the excessive naturalism that has pervaded—and blighted—much of the twentieth century. For both writers, satirical essay, romance, and prose apologetic were their main literary forms and their enduring legacies" (p. 10).

Barfield, Owen. *Owen Barfield on C. S. Lewis*. Edited by G. B. Tennyson. Middletown, Conn.: Wesleyan University Press, 1989. This is a collection of Owen Barfield's addresses, essays, and interviews about Lewis. Barfield, Lewis's friend and personal solicitor, records his personal reminiscences and critiques of Lewis's writings and thought. Speaking of *Regress* and *Surprised by Joy,* Barfield writes: "The longing was a basic element, throughout his life, in the whole man, C. S. Lewis, and forms the link between his early poems and the matured Christian philosophy of his final years" (p. 56). In a critical essay on historicism, Barfield writes of a conversation when Lewis mentioned that in painting the allegorical figure of History in book 8, chapter 8 of *Regress*, Lewis had Barfield "somewhere at the back of his mind" (p. 73).

Beversluis, John. *C. S. Lewis and the Search for Rational Religion*. Grand Rapids, Mich.: William B. Eerdmans Publishing, 1985. This author writes from a philosophical rather than a literary perspective, yet criticizes *Regress* on both levels as an "embarrassing work" which is "lackluster as fiction" and "even less successful as philosophy" (p. 10). Beversluis objects to Lewis's cavalier treatment of opposing philosophical positions and pronounces *Regress* "a gratuitously censorious little book," a "failure," and an "apprentice work" (p. 11). Ironically, this censorious critique was printed by the very publisher that prints and holds publication rights to *Regress*.

"Books." *Bulletin of the New York C. S. Lewis Society* 2 (February 1971): 15–16. An anonymous compiler, perhaps editor Henry Noel, lists sixty-two books mentioned or alluded to in *Regress*.

Bunyan, John. *The Pilgrim's Progress from This World to That Which Is to Come*. New York: Lancer Books, Magnum Easy Eye Books, 1968. Numerous publishers, reprints, and editions. (An extraordinarily large and handsome edition was published by Books for Christians of Charlotte, North Carolina, in 1972.) This allegory was first published in complete form in 1678 and is presented as a sleeping dream by the author. The main character, Christian, has a burden on his back and learns that the City of Destruction where he lives will be destroyed by fire. Part one describes his pilgrimage through the Slough of Despond, the Valley of Humiliation, the Valley of the Shadow of Death, Vanity Fair, Doubting Castle, the Delectable Mountains, the country of Beulah, and finally the Celestial City. During his travels, he encounters various allegorical personages: Mr. Worldly Wiseman, Faithful, Hopeful, Giant Despair, and Apollyon. The story is remarkable for its sustained and successful use of allegory to vividly portray abstract ideas. Lewis quotes from Bunyan at the beginning of book 7 in *Regress:* "Some also have wished that the next way to their Father's house were here that they might be troubled no more with either Hills or Mountains to go over; but the way is the way, and there's an end" (p. 103). The landscape in *Pilgrim's Progress* is revisited in 1843 by Nathaniel Hawthorne in "The Celestial Railroad."

Carnell, Corbin Scott. *Bright Shadow of Reality: C. S. Lewis and the Feeling Intellect*. Grand Rapids, Mich.: William B. Eerdmans Publishing, 1974. In this clear book-length study of *Sehnsucht,* Carnell differentiates between *Sehnsucht* and Romanticism, explaining their connection. "With the guidance particularly of *The Pilgrim's Regress* and *Surprised by Joy,* I turn now to a consideration of Lewis' early life, which will follow his awareness of *Sehnsucht* up to his late twenties, when he underwent an experience which was to alter all his future interpretations of that 'sense of separation from what is desired, that longing which always points beyond' " (p. 33). Carnell continues to refer to *Regress* throughout his study.

Christopher, Joe R. *C. S. Lewis*. Boston: G. K. Hall & Co., Twayne, 1987. In his autobiography section, before his overviews of *Surprised by Joy* and *A Grief Observed,* Christopher provides an unusually succinct and perceptive overview of *Pilgrim's Regress.* According to Christopher, Lewis wrote these three books in the tradition of Saint Augustine's *Confessions,* as an aid to later Christians. "Probably the work most like *[Pilgrim's Regress]* in the history of English literature is not Bunyan's book but William Langland's fourteenth-century poem, *Piers Plowman.* Langland has the same mixture, if not quite the same proportions, of social satire, intellectual discussion, and religious vision. (This is not an argument of influence: the similarity is one of human experience.)" Christopher's overview of *Pilgrim's Regress* is enriched with a variety of valuable details and generalities. Among the latter, he points out that John represents Lewis's Romantic position and Vertue represents his moral position. "Since Lewis held both romantic and moral positions, this sounds like a split personality; but John, the view-point character, has not yet accepted the [moral] rules of [natural law]." Unlike some other critics, Christopher values the discourses of Wisdom and History. He concludes by observing, "Indeed, the number of motifs and ideas in *The Pilgrim's Regress* that reappear in Lewis's later works indicates both how quickly his ideas matured and how little they changed."

Como, James T. "Within the Realm of Plentitude." In *C. S. Lewis at the Breakfast Table and Other Reminiscences,* edited by James T. Como. New York: Macmillan, 1979. Rev. ed., xxi–xxxiv. San Diego: Harcourt, Brace & Co., Harvest, 1992. In his introduction to a collection of essays on Lewis, Como mentions that *Regress* is "tautly structured, compulsively thorough (and autobiographical), dogmatic, and belligerent beyond any other Christian work [Lewis] was ever to write" (p. xxiv).

Cunningham, Richard B. *C. S. Lewis: Defender of the Faith*. Philadelphia: Westminster Press, 1967. According to Henry Noel, this book is perhaps the best penetration into *Regress* for its time. Cunningham writes, "While many of his allegorical images are indeed obscure, others are incisively drawn. Despite its defects, the book's importance is not to be disregarded. . . . It is one of Lewis's best books for a penetrating critique of various modern movements and thought. . . . The truth of the book becomes more profound after the second or third reading" (p. 158). Cunningham also commends Lewis for his compelling allegorical personification.

Dante Alighieri. *The Divine Comedy*. Many editions and translations. This medieval allegory includes *The Inferno, Purgatory,* and *Paradise*. Many literary allusions to the *Comedy* are found in *Regress*. A prose translation (such as P. H. Wicksteed, 1899, or H. F. Tozer, 1904) may be the best for following the story. Dorothy Sayers' *terza rima* translation has outstanding notes and maps. Along with several allusions, Lewis quotes Dante's *Comedy* on the first page of book 2 of *Regress:* "Following false copies of the good, that no / Sincere fulfilment of their promise make." Lewis also quotes the *Comedy* on the first page of book 7: "Through this and through no other fault we fell, / Nor, being fallen, bear other pain than this, / —Always without hope in desire to dwell" (canto 4 of *Inferno*). The House of Wisdom in book 7, chapter 8 of *Regress* resembles Limbo on the edge of the great pit. There on a green meadow Dante came to the wise and virtuous pagans: "You don't ask who these are? I want you to know, before you go any farther, that they were not evildoers. Although they were virtuous, that was not enough, because they were not baptised into the Christian faith. Some, living before Christianity, did not worship God adequately, and I am one of these. For such faults and no other, we are lost; and this is our only suffering: to be cut off from all hope, yet to live on in desire" (canto 4 of *Inferno*, unpublished prose translation by Kathryn Lindskoog).

Duriez, Colin, comp. *The C. S. Lewis Handbook: A Comprehensive Guide to His Life, Thought, and Writings*. Grand Rapids, Mich.: Baker Book House, 1990. In his two-page alphabetical entry for *Regress*, Duriez concludes, "It is best to enjoy the book as a story and not be too concerned with the meaning of every allusion. Read as a quest for joy, and in parallel with *Surprised by Joy*, it yields its main meanings" (p. 164). *Regress* is cross-referenced under *joy*, but unlike Lewis's other fiction, none of its characters or places are listed in the handbook.

Glover, Donald E. *C. S. Lewis: The Art of Enchantment*. Athens, Ohio: Ohio University Press, 1981. Glover's nine-page dismissal of *Regress* grants the quality of Lewis's descriptive talent, humor, and irony, but that is all. He claims that Lewis discounted the significance of *Regress* and that even the most ardent admirers of his other works have almost universally disregarded this one. He says that Lewis intended to focus more attention on the structure than on the content. Glover charges "the book is boring" and "fails to capture the reader's imagination," then concludes, "Perhaps the method, which is antiquated and traditional, has something to do with putting the reader off" (p. 68). He then suggests allegory often casts a pall upon fiction and pronounces *Regress* "a dull book" (p. 68). Glover objects to both the absence and presence of Lewis's headlines: "The allegory without the headlines is often obscure, and frequently with them, too obvious. This observation draws attention to one major failing of the book: its attention to topical and personal matters" (p. 68). Later he states, "The narration falls awkwardly upon the shoulders of this dreamer, John, who often stands in the way of narrative progress. . . . Excitement and suspense are minimal" (p. 70). Glover states *Regress* lacks "individuality and originality" and is "dry and old-fashioned" and "blatant allegory and moralizing" (p. 73).

Green, Roger Lancelyn, and Walter Hooper. *C. S. Lewis: A Biography.* London: Collins, 1974; New York: Harcourt Brace Jovanovich, 1974. Rev. ed. San Diego: Harcourt, Brace & Co., Harvest, 1994. Hooper and Green present three pages of background about the writing, publishing, and reception of *Regress*. They also present the first twelve lines of a thirty-four line unpublished poem Lewis included in a 6 May 1932 letter to Owen Barfield (p. 127). These autobiographical lines about an allegorical voyage predate the writing of *Regress*. The poem was intended to explain Lewis's conversion to Christianity and may be viewed in the Wade Center in Wheaton, Illinois, or the Bodleian Library, Oxford. The Lewis literary estate did not grant permission for publication of the poem in this guidebook to *Regress*.

Green, Roger Lancelyn. "In the Evening." In *C. S. Lewis at the Breakfast Table and Other Reminiscences,* edited by James T. Como. New York: Macmillan, 1979. Rev. ed., 210–214. San Diego: Harcourt, Brace & Co., Harvest, 1992. A lifelong friend and Lewis's chosen biographer, Green believes the brown girls in Lewis's *Regress* represent "solitary vice and unchaste thoughts" (p. 213). Green also points out a dream about a dark-skinned girl in Lewis's diary entry of 26 April 1922 and suggests a relevant connection to the brown girls in *Regress*.

Hannay, Margaret. *C. S. Lewis*. New York: Frederick Ungar Publishing, 1981. Hannay devotes four and a half pages to an accurate summary of *Regress*, and places it in the apologetics section rather than the adult fiction section. Her only criticism is of Lewis's brown girl symbolism: "There is no way to escape the implicit racism" (p. 190). In her discussion of *The Great Divorce*, without mentioning *Regress*, Hannay encapsulates the nature of dream vision literature: "Using this convention of dream and awakening is a convenient way to escape the necessity for realism in fiction without losing the reader's 'willing suspension of disbelief.' Lewis cannot expect his readers to believe that a bus runs between heaven and hell; he can expect them to believe that he had such a dream" (p. 111).

Hawthorne, Nathaniel. "The Celestial Railroad." In *Mosses from an Old Manse* (many publishers), 1846. Reprinted in *The Portable Hawthorne*, ed. Malcolm Cowley (New York: Viking Press, 1969), 242–62. Hawthorne's brief 1843 satirical sequel to John Bunyan's *Pilgrim's Progress* (1678) describes an allegorical train ride from Bunyan's City of Destruction to the Celestial City. With Mr. Smooth-it-away as his guide, Hawthorne discovers major changes that have occurred in the past 165 years; the railroad and other technology have seemingly eliminated the rigors and demands of the journey. "It is a great though incidental advantage that the materials from the heart of the Hill Difficulty have been employed in filling up the Valley of Humiliation, thus obviating the necessity of descending into that disagreeable and unwholesome hollow" (p. 248). At the beginning of book 7 of *Regress*, Lewis quotes Bunyan's *Pilgrim's Progress* on the difficulty of Hills and Mountains: "Some also have wished that the next way to their Father's house were here that they might be troubled no more with either Hills or Mountains to go over; but the way is the way, and there's an end" (p. 103). In Hawthorne's "Celestial Railroad," located at the end of the Valley of the Shadow of Death, there dwells a Giant Transcendentalist who is a German by birth. He casts honest travelers into a cave to fatten them for his table with "plentiful meals of smoke, mist, moonshine, raw potatoes, and sawdust" (p. 252). The description of this giant closely resembles Lewis's giant

"Spirit of the Age" in *Regress*. "The Celestial Railroad" may also have contributed to Lewis's idea of the bus ride from hell to heaven in *The Great Divorce* (1945).

Hodgens, Richard M. "A Note on the Brown Girl." *Bulletin of the New York C. S. Lewis Society* 17 (May 1986): 1–3. Hodgens contends the brown girl in *Regress* is borrowed from English ballad literature and does not represent a real woman.

Kaufmann, U. Milo. "*The Pilgrim's Progress* and *The Pilgrim's Regress:* John Bunyan and C. S. Lewis on the Shape of the Christian Quest." In *Bunyan in Our Time,* edited by Robert G. Collmer, 186–99. Kent, Ohio: Kent State University Press, 1989. Kaufmann examines the contrasting elements of Christian's one-way flight from the world to heaven and John's two-way journey. John's quest consists of a response to a call from beyond this world (longing or *Sehnsucht*) and a "regress or return from the world's edge into the community of men for witness and redemptive work" (p. 294).

Kilby, Clyde S. *The Christian World of C. S. Lewis*. Grand Rapids, Mich.: William B. Eerdmans Publishing, 1964. With deep affection for Lewis, Kilby writes warmly of *Regress* and devotes pages 25–36 to summary and discussion of the allegorical representations. Although a difficult book to understand, "it will reward anyone who is willing to stay with it, and will in fact grow increasingly meaningful as one contemplates the spiritual significance of such remarks" (p. 35). On the same page Kilby mistakes Slikisteinsauga, one of the Landlord's mountain children in book 9, chapter 6 of *Regress,* for the Holy Spirit, despite conversation that makes it clear he is a guardian angel.

———. *Images of Salvation in the Fiction of C. S. Lewis*. Wheaton, Ill.: Harold Shaw Publishers, 1978. In this book Kilby devotes an entire chapter to *Regress* and, after a summary, offers an examination of the allegorical meaning. The author provides a translation of many foreign expressions in *Regress*.

———, ed. *A Mind Awake: An Anthology of C. S. Lewis*. New York: Harcourt, Brace & World, 1969. Although it includes only a few passages from *Regress,* Kilby's anthology is useful for readers interested in further reading on particular themes. The anthology contains a wide selection from Lewis's fiction and nonfiction, essays, book reviews, poetry, and letters.

Knight, Gareth. *The Magical World of the Inklings: J. R. R. Tolkien, C. S. Lewis, Charles Williams, Owen Barfield.* Longmead, G.B.: Element Books, 1990. Knight calls *Regress* a " 'donnish' allegorical account" and "a fascinating example of modern allegory" (pp. 5, 17). In discussing the districts on Lewis's *Regress* map, Knight points out that Lewis's friend Charles Williams "wandered in the region of Occultica, Behmenheim and Glamoria, perhaps coming perilously close to the town of Magopolis, the centre of cult leaders and power-hungry magicians" (p. 18).

Kreeft, Peter. *C. S. Lewis: A Critical Essay.* Grand Rapids, Mich.: William B. Eerdmans Publishing, 1969. This forty-eight page monograph deals only in passing with *Regress.* Kreeft inaccurately writes that Lewis labeled *Regress* "his worst book" (p. 6). He also criticizes "the wooden technique . . . and small-minded name-calling" of *Regress* (p. 9).

Lindskoog, Kathryn. *The C. S. Lewis Hoax.* Portland, Oreg.: Multnomah Press, 1988. This book brings to light many disturbing questions regarding the authenticity, editing, and provenance of many posthumous works attributed to C. S. Lewis. The inordinately careless text notes in the Bantam edition of *Regress* are mentioned (pp. 78–79).

———. *Light in the Shadowlands: Protecting the Real C. S. Lewis.* Sisters, Oreg.: Multnomah Books, 1994. Although this book focuses on the falsity of some of the information injected into C. S. Lewis's life story since his death, and the falsity of some inferior literature published under his name since his death, chapter 5 rescues from oblivion a fascinating novel that Lewis began five years before he wrote *Regress.* This ironic 5,330-word pre-Christian fragment, "The Most Substantial People," foreshadows *Regress* by featuring a character obsessed with a terror of hell (like John) and a character obsessed with "the good life" (like the insubstantial Mr. Sensible). "The Most Substantial People" can only be read in the Lewis family papers in the Wade Center or the Bodleian Library, but Lindskoog has closely paraphrased it in its entirety for readers. Lindskoog also points out that in the Bantam annotated edition of *Regress* Dr. John C. Traupman chose thirty phrases to identify in endnotes, then designated nineteen of them "Source unknown."

———. *The Lion of Judah in Never-Never Land: The Theology of C. S. Lewis Expressed in His Fantasies for Children.* Grand Rapids, Mich.: William B. Eerdmans Publishing, 1973. (Scheduled for republication in a collection titled *Journey into Narnia*.) C. S. Lewis responded warmly to this 957 master's thesis, published in 1973, in which Lindskoog analyzes his core beliefs about philosophy, theology, psychology, and sociology in the *Chronicles of Narnia* and his previous writings. She draws upon *Regress* and ends her book with a passage from *Regress* preceded by this statement: "These three concepts [Lewis's opinions about nature, mankind, and God] have been graphically presented in mythological form in the Narnian tales.

"Lewis expressed his feeling about mythology in relation to Christianity in *The Pilgrim's Regress,* the first book he wrote after becoming a Christian. *This book has never enjoyed the popularity of many of his later works, but it was the source of the ideas in most of them*" (p. 129, italics added). After reading her manuscript, Lewis responded in a handwritten letter dated 29 October 1957: "Your thesis arrived yesterday and I read it at once. You are in the center of the target everywhere. For one thing, you know my work better than anyone else I've met; certainly better than I do myself. . . . But secondly you (alone of the critics I've met) realize the connection, or even the unity, of all the books—scholarly, fantastic, theological—and make me appear a single author not a man who impersonates half a dozen authors, which is what I seem to most. This wins really very high marks indeed. . . . If you understand me so well you will understand other authors too. I hope we shall have some really useful critical works from your hand. With thanks and good wishes."

Manlove, C. N. *C. S. Lewis: His Literary Achievement.* New York: St. Martin's Press, 1987. Manlove devotes an entire chapter to *Regress* and discusses its imagery and theological implications. He argues that its main weakness is in the allegory. He commends Lewis because the book begins "brilliantly with a child's trauma about masks, rules and a black hole so profoundly stamped on his personality that they colour his experience throughout his life" (p. 15). This accounts for John's ongoing terror of the Landlord.

Meilaender, Gilbert. *The Taste for the Other: The Social and Ethical Thought of C. S. Lewis.* Grand Rapids, Mich.: William B. Eerdmans Publishing, 1978. This book is a detailed presentation of the theology in Lewis's writings. Avoiding stuffy theological discussion, Meilaender emphasizes practical application and shows a deep understanding of *Regress.* He writes, "The key to *[Regress],* for Lewis, is its central element: incarnation. Hence, to enter the story and understand one's life by it is not to seek holiness but to follow Christ—to respond to the lure of his call" (p. 39). He concludes that the social and ethical themes in Lewis's writings are Augustinian, thus generally acceptable to both Catholics and Protestants.

Myers, Doris T. *C. S. Lewis in Context.* Kent, Ohio: Kent State University Press, 1994. Myers' narrowly focused fifteen-page essay "Two Kinds of Metaphor in *The Pilgrim's Regress*" is the most scholarly and detailed analysis of *Regress* to date. Approaching Lewis's fiction through the linguistic controversies and "language cynicism" that followed World War I, Myers begins by explaining that Lewis first attempted to defend Christianity by showing that in the postwar period the intellectuals' reasons for rejecting traditional literature and Christianity were based on illusion. She divides Lewis's metaphors into two kinds: archetypal (geography, weather, seasons, "archetypal figures") and personal (cities, homes, artifacts, "humor characters"). With a fine eye for twentieth-century follies, Lewis addressed contemporary literature, philosophy, and religion. According to Myers, Lewis satirized three types of Anglican churchmanship: the Anglo-Catholic (Mr. Angular), the evangelical (the Steward), and the broad (Mr. Broad). Myers concludes that *Regress* is worth reading, especially for the inherent power in images and metaphors that Lewis would repeat and develop in his subsequent fiction.

Noel, Henry. "A Guide to C. S. Lewis's *The Pilgrim's Regress.*" *Bulletin of the New York C. S. Lewis Society* 2 (February 1971): 4–15. In the most comprehensive yet concise article on *Regress,* Henry Noel correlates Lewis's conversion in his autobiographical account *Surprised by Joy* with *Regress.* He lists characters in the allegory and their meanings. He defines all the foreign terms in *Regress* and concludes his essay with excerpts from early reviews.

Ostling, Joan K. "A Forthcoming Annotated Bibliography of C. S. Lewis." *Bulletin of the New York C. S. Lewis Society* 2 (February 1971): 3. Ostling's list of ten reviews of *Regress* supplements Henry Noel's "A Guide to C. S. Lewis's *The Pilgrim's Regress*" in the same issue of the *Bulletin*.

Peters, John. *C. S. Lewis: The Man and His Achievement*. Exeter, Eng.: Paternoster Press, 1985. Peters devotes an entire twenty-page chapter to *Regress*, with warm-hearted analysis more pastoral than academic. Only two of his judgments are highly questionable: that the genesis of *Regress* was Lewis's first draft of his poem about Lilith in a letter to Arthur Greeves dated 29 April 1930, and that Mr. Neo-Angular represents Catholicism. Peters declares, "[Lewis's] prose is typically enchanting and lucid, and it can be argued that *The Pilgrim's Regress* is as remarkable and important as any of his other works. Yet it has been curiously neglected—in the long and short term—both by the general public and by Lewis devotees." He gives a variety of reasons for its neglect, then a variety of reasons for its importance. He concludes: "Fashions—philosophical, political and sociological—and personalities have inevitably changed since 1933, but not the abiding significance of traditional Christianity for a world divided by ideological and economic barriers." He adds that *Regress* "is a powerful antidote and corrective, and it deserves to be re-discovered and enjoyed. It does not—it must be admitted—yield its pearls easily, and there are places where Lewis is either too heavy or too complex, but it does repay the discriminating and persevering reader" (p. 49). He notes that *Regress* was the work which launched Lewis "into the world of the professional theologian, because it brought him to the attention of Dr. Alex Vidler, then editor of the monthly journal *Theology*" (p. 50). Vidler invited Lewis to become a contributor, which led to many lively exchanges, including such notable papers as "Christianity and Culture."

Piehler, Paul. "Myth or Allegory? Archetype and Transcendence in the Fiction of C. S. Lewis." In *Word and Story in C. S. Lewis,* edited by Peter J. Schakel and Charles A. Huttar, 199–212. Columbia, Mo.: University of Missouri Press, 1991. Piehler examines Lewis's use of the great medieval visionary allegories in his fiction, particularly *Regress*. He defines two types of allegory: (1) Allegory of Vision, which reaches after myth, archetype and transcendence, and (2) Allegory of Demystification, which turns away from evoking spiritual realities. *Regress* and Prudentius's fourth-century *Psychomachia* are grouped together as examples of the second type. According to Piehler *Regress* is "a highly successful, indeed brilliant, work." Nevertheless, it "merits no more than its relatively minor place in the Lewis canon." Piehler offers as evidence only Lewis's comments in the 1943 preface (p. 203).

Reilly, R. J. *Romantic Religion: A Study of Barfield, Lewis, Williams, and Tolkien.* Athens, Ga.: University of Georgia Press, 1971. Reilly aims to show "the progress of a certain sort of romantic imagination from irreligion into Christianity, and show further that the characteristic work produced by the baptized romantic imagination is baptized romance" (p. 100). He claims that when the book *Phantastes* baptized C. S. Lewis's imagination, it raised *Sehnsucht* to religious awe, and then it was up to Lewis to determine "whether any present religion was the 'true' religion" (p. 103). At this point Reilly turns briefly to *Regress*. In passing, he misidentifies the Landlord's castle as the Church, and erroneously claims that John moved all the way North into the land of Fascism and Marxian Communism.

Routley, Erik. "A Prophet." In *C. S. Lewis at the Breakfast Table and Other Reminiscences,* edited by James T. Como. New York: Macmillan, 1979. Rev. ed., 33–37. San Diego: Harcourt, Brace & Co., Harvest, 1992. Routley, an undergraduate at Magdalen College during World War II, speaks very highly of *Regress:* "I do want to express the hope that you people know and value one of Lewis's earliest Christian works, *The Pilgrim's Regress.* . . . My final memory of those otherwise dim Oxford days is sitting up unto the small hours night after night with the first edition of that book—the one without the preface and the running headline—working out what it was all about: getting inside his 'north-south' pattern and understanding all the allegorical references on every page. . . . We took some satisfaction, when the explained edition came out, in finding that we had pretty well got it right" (p. 36).

Sayer, George. *Jack: C. S. Lewis and His Times.* San Francisco: Harper & Row, 1988. Reissued, with an afterword, as *Jack: A Life of C. S. Lewis,* Wheaton, Ill.: Crossway Books, 1994. Sayer, a personal friend of Lewis's for many years, has written what may become the definitive biography of Lewis. Sayer praises *Regress* for its "captivating freshness," then adds, "No other book of his is written with such a light touch, and few are so often witty and profound" (p. 136). He commends Lewis's "tutor's gift for presenting complex ideas in simple form" and adds that the last sections of *Regress* rise to "mystical heights" (p. 136). In particular, Sayer praises and quotes from the last paragraph of book 9, chapter 5 because it "rises to the greatness of the theme" (p. 136).

Sayers, Dorothy. "The Writing and Reading of Allegory." In *The Whimsical Christian: 18 Essays*, 205–34. New York: Macmillan, 1978. Sayers presents a modern defense of allegory as an important literary genre and contends that today's readers lack a basic understanding and enjoyment of allegory. She provides a brief history of the use of allegory by Ovid, Chaucer, Dante, Spenser, Bunyan, Tennyson, and Kafka, and argues that the allegorical method has been employed in the language of psychoanalysis. She contends that a resurrection of allegory as a literary device accompanies each profound change in culture (i.e., the twelfth-century discovery of romantic love). She then identifies allegory's purpose: to personify an abstract psychological experience so as to make it more vivid and comprehensible. Her advice on reading allegory is excellent preparatory reading for any allegory, and this essay should be included in any collection of critical essays on *Regress*.

Schakel, Peter J. *Reason and Imagination in C. S. Lewis: A Study of "Till We Have Faces."* Grand Rapids, Mich.: William B. Eerdmans Publishing, 1984. In his study of Lewis's last novel, *Till We Have Faces*, Schakel points out imagery common to this book and *Regress,* including masks, clothing, sight, and veils. In contrasting the two works Schakel notes that *Regress* emphasizes "the acceptance of Christianity by the understanding and the will; myth and imagination are much less important than they will be in *Till We Have Faces*" (p. 121). He criticizes *Regress* as allegory: Lewis "is unable to embody his material in images and events sufficiently to make it directly apprehendable by the imagination" (p. 121). This book provides an analysis of the explicit comments on myth in *Regress,* Lewis's essay "Myth Became Fact," and a letter from Lewis to Greeves discussing the nature of myth. Schakel concludes: "Myth, in the terms of *The Pilgrim's Regress,* is neither 'fact' (the scientific or historical—dealt with by reason) nor 'the very real (the concrete—apprehended by the senses); it is, rather, 'truth' or 'an image'—to be grasped with the imagination" (p. 124).

Spenser, Edmund. *The Faerie Queene*. Books 1–3, 1590; Books 4–6, 1596. Numerous editions. Spenser wrote his book-length poem *The Faerie Queene* in the stanza pattern he invented. His poem is composed of six books containing moral, religious, historical, and political allegory. Episodes such as Sir Guyon's visit to the cave of Mammon, or his temptation by the Lady of the Idle Lake, bear some resemblance to parts of *Pilgrim's Progress* and Lewis's *Regress*. The Queen (who allegorically signifies glory) has twelve knights (examples of twelve different virtues). Each knight undertakes an adventure. Prince Arthur represents magnificence and the Redcrosse Knight of Holiness is the Anglican Church. The Virgin Una represents truth or true religion. Lewis quotes Spenser in the beginning of book 2 of *Regress:* "In hand she boldly took / To make another like the former dame, / Another Florimell in shape and look / So lively and so like that many it mistook" (p. 17).

Vanauken, Sheldon. *A Severe Mercy*. San Francisco: Harper & Row, 1977. An autobiographical account of love, marriage, conversion to Christianity, loss, and grief. Through the influence of Lewis, Sheldon and Jean Vanauken became believers. The book contains eighteen personal letters from Lewis.

Walsh, Chad. *C. S. Lewis: Apostle to the Skeptics*. New York: Macmillan, 1949. Although Walsh is an outstanding guide to Lewis in most respects, he calls *Regress* "mediocre" and states that only one poem "lingers strongly" in his mind (pp. 49, 61). He claims that *Regress* is "interesting mainly to the scholar bent upon *Quellenforschung* (source research)" and that it is "heavy, complex, [and] obscure" (p. 158).

———. *The Literary Legacy of C. S. Lewis*. New York: Harcourt Brace Jovanovich, 1979. In his brief discussion of *Regress,* Walsh expresses a lack of appreciation for allegory in general: "*The Pilgrim's Regress* suffers from vices that also infest Bunyan's book, and indeed any allegory. If the characters in a tale exist only to symbolize and embody particular beliefs and attitudes, they can hardly take on living personality; they are abstract nouns spelled with capital letters" (p. 62). His appraisal of *Regress* is consistently negative.

White, William Luther. *The Image of Man in C. S. Lewis.* Nashville: Abingdon Press, 1969. White claims that *Regress* is Lewis's "imaginative work which displays the most concern over Joy" (p. 115). White offers no personal appraisal of *Regress,* but shows a good understanding of its themes and similar themes throughout Lewis's other writings.

Wilson, A. N. *C. S. Lewis: A Biography.* New York: W. W. Norton & Co., 1990. Wilson's biography is riddled throughout with significant inaccuracies. His pages sparkle with a mix of good information, errors, and falsehoods demeaning Lewis's faith. He has mixed feelings about *Regress:* its "contemporary references seem crude and dead as mutton . . . yet, the book's virtues greatly outweigh its faults" (p. 134). Wilson inexplicably misidentifies Victoriana with John Betjeman. He credits Lewis with "tremendous narrative verve . . . flights of true sublimity . . . [and] knockabout . . . comedy and debate" (p. 135).

# INDEX

*Regress* book titles are set in ALL CAPITALS, and chapter titles are set in SMALL CAPITALS.

*Abolition of Man, The* 133
Absolute Idealism xix–xx, 69, 84, 87
ACROSS THE CANYON 92–99
ACROSS THE CANYON 97–98
ACROSS THE CANYON BY MOONLIGHT 73–74
ACROSS THE CANYON BY THE INNER LIGHT 93
"Adam at Night" 46
Alexander, Samuel 8
allegory xvi, xx, xxiv, xxvii, xxxiii, 22, 49, 115–122
*Allegory of Love, The* 115–16, 121, 132
Anglo-Catholicism 61
Angular, Mr. 58, 60–63, 65, 97
Anthroposophical Society 78
Apostate Bishop 17
Arcadia 21, 50
ARCHTYPE AND ECTYPE 38–40, 91
Aristotle 53, 82, 104
*Art* 18
Aslan 33, 41, 119
AT BAY 83–91

"Auguries of Innocence" 72
Augustine, Saint 95, 102
"Aunt and Amabel, The" 9

*Babbitt* 21
BACK TO THE ROAD 37–42
Barfield, Owen xxi, xxiii, xxv–xxvi, xxxii, 22, 78, 96
BBC Radio xxxiii, 122
Bell, Clive 18
Berkeley, George 40, 80
*Beyond Personality* 133
BLACK HOLE, THE 104
Blake, William 72–73
*Book of Common Prayer, The* 105, 110
*Book of the Duchess* xxvii
Broad, Mr. 69, 71–73
BROOK, THE 109–114
brown girl(s), the 1, 10, 19–21, 27, 39, 86
Bunyan, John xxiii, xxvii, xxix, xxxiii, 75, 78–79, 119, 121–22

Carroll, Lewis 34

## 162 INDEX

CAUGHT 86–87
"Celestial Railroad, The" 78
Chaucer, Geoffrey xxvii
Chesterton, G. K. 7
*Christian Reflections* 15, 98
"Christianity and Culture " 15, 18
Christopher, Joe 74
*Chronicles of Narnia, The* 119, 127, 133
Claptrap 13, 15, 60, 77
Classical 58, 60–61, 65
Clevers, the 24–27, 29–30, 62, 87
"Confession, A" 26
Cowper, William 54
*Crock of Gold, The* 110

Dante Alighieri xxvii, 16, 75, 87–88, 90, 98, 102, 107, 116–17
DATA, THE 1–11
"Death in Battle" xix
Dirty Twenties 28
*Divine Comedy, The* xxvii, 87, 90, 98, 116
DIXIT INSIPIENS 14–15
"Dogma and the Universe" 15
Donne, John 20, 114
dream narrative xxvii
DRUDGE 44, 55–56, 58–60, 64–65
Dufflepuds 26
*Dymer* xx, xxviii, xxxi, 132

EASTERN MOUNTAINS, THE 6–8
eastern mountain(s) 6, 16, 31, 99–100
*Eclogues* 50, 52
Eliot, T. S. 26, 61–62, 113–14
Emerson, Ralph Waldo 80
Enlightenment, Mr. 13–15, 31, 39, 60, 71
Enlightenment, Sigismund 25, 31
Epichaerecacia 60
*Epistles* 50, 52

ESCAPE 41–42
ESCHROPOLIS 25–26
Eschropolis 21, 30, 60, 62
*Essay Concerning Human Understanding* 38
ESSE IS PERCIPI 40–41
ESSENCE OF ALLEGORY, THE 115–22
*Everlasting Man* 7
Existential, Mr. 48
"Extasie, The" 20

FACING THE FACTS 32–33
*Faerie Queene, The* 37, 116–17, 120
FIRST STEPS TO THE NORTH 59
FOOD AT A COST 86
FOOD FROM THE NORTH 64
FOOLS' PARADISE 65–67
*Four Loves, The* 39, 133
*Four Quartets* 113
Fowler, Dr. Alastair 120
FREEDOM OF THOUGHT 28–30
Freud, Sigmund 31
Freudian 24, 31–32, 38, 42
"Funeral of a Great Myth, The" 15
FURTHEST NORTH 64–65

GAUCHERIE OF VERTUE, THE 55–56
Geoffrey Bles Publishers xxx, xxxii
*Georgics* 50, 53–54
GIANT SLAYER, THE 34–35
Glugly 25, 29
GOING SOUTH 71
*Golden Key, The* 96
GRAND CANYON, THE 44–56
*Great Divorce, The* xxvii, 17, 72, 82, 119, 121, 133
GREAT PROMISES 21–22
Green, Roger Lancelyn 9–10
Greeves, Arthur xv–xviii, xxi–xxiv, xxvi–xxviii, 14, 16, 18, 25, 48–49, 73, 89, 96, 100, 105, 108, 132

*Grief Observed, A* 133
Griffiths, Alan Bede xxxi–xxxii, 59, 66, 82, 90

Halfways, Gus 13, 20–22, 24–25, 30, 59
Halfways, Media 13, 17–21, 60, 65
Halfways, Mr. 13, 18–19, 25, 30, 60
Hamilton, Clive xxiii
Havard, Robert E. 66–67
Hawthorne, Nathaniel 78–79
Henley, William Ernest 47–48
Herbert, George 46
HERMIT, THE 87–88
HILL, THE 16–17
HISTORY'S WORDS 88–89
Homer xxv
Hopkins, Gerard Manley 94
Horace 50–52, 54
*Horse and His Boy, The* 88
*House of Fame, The* xxvii
HOUSE OF WISDOM, THE 75
Humanist 58, 60, 62, 64–65
"Hymn to God My God, in My Sickness" 114

ICHABOD 10, 20
IGNORANTIA 106
*In Darkest Africa* 24, 32
*Inferno, The* 16, 75, 107
Island, the 2, 4–6, 8, 21, 25, 31, 38–39, 62–63, 73–74, 76, 92, 98

JOHN FINDS HIS VOICE 85
JOHN FORGETS HIMSELF 85
JOHN LEADING 70–71
JOHN LED 84
Joy xv–xvi, xix–xx, xxiv, xxxi, 2, 4–5, 8, 10, 38, 90

Kant, Immanuel 78
Keats, John 19

Kilby, Clyde 29, 54, 79
Kreeft, Peter xxxi

Landlord 2–4, 6, 13, 19, 39, 42, 45, 74–76, 85–90, 92, 98–99, 104–105
*Last Battle, The* 37
Lawrence, D. H. 27
LEAH FOR RACHEL 8–10, 19
L'Engle, Madeleine 126
LET GRILL BE GRILL 37–38
Lewis, Sinclair 21
Lewis, Warren H. xiv, xxiv, xxx, 3, 66, 131–32
*Light Princess, The* 77
LIMBO 102–3
*Lion, the Witch and the Wardrobe, The* 9
*Literary Legacy of C. S. Lewis, The* 22
LITTLE SOUTHWARD, A 17–18
Locke, John 38, 40
"Love Song of J. Alfred Prufrock, The" 26
Luther, Martin 53
LUXURIA 107–8

*Macbeth* 101
MacDonald, George xvi, xxii, 73, 77, 96, 103, 132
Maddocks, Melvin 29
Main Road xxi, 13, 22, 42, 45
MAIN ROAD AGAIN, THE 71
Mammon, Mr. 25, 30, 87
MAN BEHIND THE GUN, THE 30
Mappa Mundi 16
Marx, Karl 64, 77
Master Parrot 25
MATTER OF FACT 89–90
Mead, Hunter 80–81
*Mere Christianity* 127
metaphysics 39, 69

*Mind of God, The* 40
*Miracles* 133
MORE WISDOM 80–82
Morris, William xxiii–xxiv
"Most Substantial People, The" 132
Mother Kirk 14, 44–45, 47–48, 62–63, 72, 77–78, 80, 82, 92, 95–96, 101
MOTHER KIRK'S STORY 45–46
MUM'S THE WORD 79
Myers, Doris T. 18
mythology 16, 88, 97, 123–24
mythology, Norse xiv–xvi, 19, 65

Narnia 9, 27, 33
NELLA SUA VOLUNTADE 98–99
NEO-ANGULAR 62–63
Neo-Classical, Mr. *See* Classical
Nesbit, Edith 9
Noel, Henry 49
NON EST HIC 20–21
NORTHERN DRAGON, THE 108
NORTHWARD ALONG THE CANYON 58–67

*Odes* 50–51, 54
*Odyssey* xxv
"On Being Human" 103
Oreads 6
*Orthodoxy* 7
*Out of the Silent Planet* 132

Palmer, Herbert Edward 25
*Parliament of Fowls* xxvii
parrot disease 33–34
*Perelandra* 97, 116, 119, 133
*Personal Heresy, The* 28, 132
Phally or Phallus 25, 27
*Phantastes* xvi
philosophy xxix, 69, 79, 82, 87
*Piers Plowman* xxvii

*Pilgrim's Progress, The* xxiii–xxiv, xxvii, xxxiii, 2, 78, 116, 121–22
*Poems* 26, 34, 46, 85–86, 91, 95, 101, 103–9, 111–12, 123
POISONING THE WELLS 31–32
Potter, Beatrix xiv
*Prince Caspian* 41
*Princess and Curdie, The* xxii
*Princess and the Goblin, The* xxii, 73
*Principles of Human Knowledge* 40
*Problem of Pain, The* 29, 132
"Prudent Jailer, The" 52
*Punch* 26, 46, 103
*Purgatory* 87–88

QUEM QUAERITIS IN SEPULCHRO? NON EST HIC 11

Reason 25, 35, 37–39, 41–42, 44, 53, 63, 70, 74, 76, 81, 92–94, 97, 120, 122, 130
REASON AND IMAGINATION 123–30
REGRESS, THE 100–114
"Religion and Science" 15
*Romance of the Rose* xxvii
RULES, THE 2–4

SAME YET DIFFERENT, THE 101
Savage 58, 65, 70, 77
Sayers, Dorothy L. 115–16
*Screwtape Letters, The* 133
SECURUS TE PROJICE 95–97
SELF-SUFFICIENCY OF VERTUE, THE 46–49
Sensible, Mr. 44, 49, 51–56, 62, 71–72, 101–2
Shakespeare, William 101–2
*Siegfried and the Twilight of the Gods* xv
*Silver Chair, The* 33

Singh, Sadhu Sundar  84
Sister Penelope  58
Sitwell, Edith  25–26
SOFT GOING  18
SOUTHERN DRAGON, THE  109
SOUTHWARD ALONG THE CANYON  69–82
SOUTH WIND, A  27–28
*Space, Time and Deity*  8
"Spartan Nactus"  26
Spencer, Herbert  77
Spenser, Edmund  37, 117–18, 120
*Spenser's Images of Life*  120–21
Spirit of the Age  24–25, 30–32, 34–35, 38–39, 41–42, 62, 70, 74, 79, 87, 129
*Spirits in Bondage*  xviii–xix, xxxi, 132
Stanley, Henry Morton  24, 31
Stephens, James  110
Stevenson, Robert Louis  17
Steward  1, 3–6, 14, 25, 47, 71, 76, 102
SUPERBIA  104–6
*Surprised by Joy*  xiv–xv, xxxii, 32, 133
SYNTHETIC MAN, THE  101–2

TABLE TALK  53–55
Tao  45
TEA ON THE LAWN  71–73
Tertullian  60
*That Hideous Strength*  15, 49, 133
*Theories of Everything*  40
THIS SIDE BY LIGHTNING  93–94
THIS SIDE BY SUNLIGHT  74–76
THIS SIDE BY THE DARKNESS  94–95
THREE PALE MEN  59–62
THRILL  13–22
thrill  xviii, 60, 63

THROUGH DARKEST ZEITGEISTHEIM  24–35
*Through the Dark Continent*  24, 32
*Through the Looking Glass*  34
*Till We Have Faces*  6, 112–13, 123–25, 127, 130, 133
Tolkien, J. R. R.  xxiii–xxiv
TWO KINDS OF MONIST  83–84

Uncle George  1, 6, 94
UNDER ARREST  30–31

Vertue  6, 13, 17, 45, 47–49, 51, 53, 55–56, 58–60, 64–65, 69–71, 73, 80, 83–84, 86, 89, 92, 99, 101, 103, 105, 109–11
VERTUE IS SICK  69–70
VICTORIANA  24–26
Virgil  50–54
*Vita Nuova*  116
*Voyage of the "Dawn Treader," The*  5, 26

Walsh, Chad  22, 48, 61–62
"Weight of Glory"  86
Williams, Charles  132
*Wind in the Willows, The*  22
Wisdom  69, 72–77, 80–83, 93, 97
WISDOM—ESOTERIC  77–79
WISDOM—EXOTERIC  76–77
*Wood between the Worlds, The*  xxiv
Wordsworth, William  xxv, 71

YEARS OF THE LIFE OF C. S. LEWIS  131–133
Yeats, William Butler  19, 132
"Your True Antiquities"  111

Zeitgeistheim  24, 27